New England Timeline

New England Timeline

A Concise Guide to the Region's History

Ron McAdow

PHP

Personal History Press
Lincoln, Massachusetts

Illustration Credits: Back cover, postal map by by H. Moll, geographer, 1732, Wikipedia Commons; John Winthrop, page 8, engraving by Girsch from painting attributed to Anthony van Dyck; page 10, Return of Roger Williams from England with the First Charter, 1644, from a painting by C.R. Grant. Engraving by Arnold Greene, 1886; page 13, Whitefield House, from A.S. Bolle's *Industrial History of the United States*, 1878; page 17, Mary Dyer statue, photo by the author; page 20, Sir Edmund Andros, English engraving, New York Public Library Digital Collection; page 20, Charter Oak, from R. U. Pipers's *The Trees of America* (1855); page 24, Narragansett Pacer, from *American Horses and Horse Breeding* by John Dimon, 1895; page 33, "Minute Man" by Danniel Chester French, 1875, photo by author: page 35, "George Washington" by Thomas Ball, photo by author; page 41, Portland Head Light, from *Historic American Buildings Survey*, 1933; page 44, Red Horse sign, photo by author; page 49, Lucy Larcom, Houghton Mifflin photo; page 51, USS *Constitution* in 1997, Navy photo by Journalist 2nd Class Todd Stevens; page 53, locomotive, John Carbutt, 1871; page 55, Fruitlands, photo by author; page 62, Ice cutters, - U.S. National Archives and Records Administration; page 63, Duryea automobile, 1890s, Wikipedia Commons; page 83, Old Manse, Historic American Buildings Survey, Photographer: Frank O. Branzetti; 1941.

Copyright 2016 Ron McAdow

ISBN: 978-0-9983619-1-8

Library of Congress Control Number: 2016931668

PHP

Personal History Press
Lincoln, Massachusetts

www.personalhistorypress.com

New England Timeline

Table of Contents

Prehistory 1

Early History 4

1700s 24

1800s 44

1900s 65

2000s 70

American Natives and English Colonists 72

New England and the War for Independence 77

Industry and Idealism 80

Maps 87

Bibliography 98

Index 101

New England Timeline

Years Before Present

15,000

The **most recent glacier retreats**. At its height the ice covered all of New England, even the tallest mountains. Because much of the planet's water was locked into continental glaciers, oceans were lower during the Ice Age, coastal harbors were dry land, and mammoths grazed on George's Bank. As the glacier melted, clay, sand, and gravel were released. The islands of Martha's Vineyard and Nantucket are glacial deposits called terminal moraines. They mark the longest reach of the next-to-last ice sheet. Cape Cod is a terminal moraine of the last glacier. Huge lakes of glacial meltwater filled many New England river valleys; sediments deposited on those lake-bottoms became the region's most productive soil.

9000+

Groups of **Paleo-Indians** hunted large mammals such as mastodon, bison, woodland caribou, and giant beaver. New England's climate resembled that of present-day northern Canada. Its vegetation gradually changed from tundra to northern forest.

9000-4000

New England was peopled by the Archaic Indians, hunter gatherers who migrated between single-season camps and use a variety of vegetable and animal foods. In the estuary of the Charles River, Archaic Indians built a fish weir, the remains of which were discovered during the construction of a Boston subway. The weir was a long fence of basketry supported by posts. The structure was flooded at high tide, but it was dry when the tide was out; fish were trapped behind the basketry as the water recedes.

Based on the quantity of artifacts this era's people left behind, the inland population peaked during this time.

2700-1000

The **Algonquians** enter New England from the Midwest, bringing with them knowledge of pottery, the bow and arrow, and agriculture. Algonquians became the dominant cultural influence, although it is unknown whether this took place through gradual assimilation or by warfare. When the Europeans arrived, all American natives from the maritime provinces to North Carolina spoke languages of the Eastern Algonquian family.

1000-500

In the **Late Woodland Period**, native farmers grew corn, beans, tobacco, and squash including pumpkins and zucchini. They made extensive use of fish, shellfish, and marine mammals; gathered berries, nuts, seeds, and roots; and hunted deer, bear, beaver, raccoon, rabbit, and muskrat. Their homes were wigwams, framed with bent saplings and covered with mats or bark.

Canoes were the principal contribution of Native Americans to transportation. In northern New England birchbark canoes were made from single sheets of bark stripped from large paper birches. Southern craftsmen made dugout canoes from large trees. English settlers purchased canoes from the Indians and found them so useful they called them "water horses."

500

Contact between Native Americans and Europeans follows the voyage of Columbus. The Abenaki (Dawn Land People) populated northern New England. Vermont and New Hampshire were the territory of the Western Abenaki, although possession of Vermont was contested by the fierce Iroquois of New York. Western Abenaki tribes are the Ossippee, Pequawket, and Winnipesauke. Eastern New Hampshire and all of Maine were Eastern Abenaki, with separate tribes occupying various river valleys—Maine's rivers were named by or for the Abenaki groups that lived alongside them.

The Pennacook occupied southern New Hampshire and included the Amoskeag, Nashua, Piscataqua, Souhegan, and Squamscot tribes. The land that will become Massachusetts was home to the Nipmuck, Pawtucket, Massachusetts, and Wampanoag. Rhode Island had mostly Narraganset but also Niantic, Nipmuck, Pequot, and Wampanoag. Connecticut's natives were Pequot, Mohegan, Tunxis, Housatonic, and Wyachtonok.

Forest management by fire was practiced by the natives in much of New England. Annual burning of the underbrush eased foot travel and encouraged food-producing plants such as strawberries, raspberries, and blackberries without destroying the oaks, hickories, and chestnuts that also generated valuable food for human beings and their prey animals.

Years C.E.

1492 **Columbus** finds the New World.

1498 **John Cabot**, hired to explore for King Henry VII, visits the northern shores of North America. England's claims to the continent were based on Cabot's "discovery."

1524 **Giovanni da Verrazzano** sails along the Atlantic Coast of North America. When he entered Narragansett Bay, he was welcomed by a score of dugout canoes containing hospitable natives who traded furs for glass jewelry.

After staying fifteen days with these Indians, Verrazzano continued up the coast, visiting Maine before returning to Europe.

1530-1600

Although North America still had no permanent settlements, Maine had numerous temporary stations where European sailors paused to trade for furs and to preserve their fish by drying. Such stations were occupied for at most a season; they did not represent attempts at colonization.

1580 **Massasoit**, sachem of the Wampanoag, was born about this time. He would become the protector and benefactor of the Plymouth Colony.

1602 **Bartholomew Gosnold** explores New England's coast in the ship *Concord*, seeking sassafras, because its fragrant roots are considered of medical value. Gosnold sailed along Maine and south to Cape Cod, which he named for the excellent fishing he found there. After harvesting sassafras and visiting the Elizabeth Islands and Martha's Vineyard, Gosnold returned to England with an enthusiastic report on the commercial potential of New England, supporting his claims with a profitable cargo.

1603 As a result of Gosnold's voyage, Martin Pring is sent to harvest two shiploads of sassafras. Pring ventured twenty miles up New Hampshire's Piscataqua River, then rounded Cape Ann and crossed Massachusetts Bay to the future site of Plymouth, where he spent seven weeks. His report of the bountiful crops of the natives encouraged the belief that Massachusetts could support a colony.

1604 From his ship in Maine's Casco Bay, French explorer **Samuel de Champlain** sees the White Mountains of New Hampshire. In the following two years Champlain completed his map of the New England coast, visiting and charting the harbors that became Gloucester, Boston, and Plymouth.

John Eliot is born in Hertfordshire, England. Eliot devoted much of his life to the welfare of Massachusetts Indians.

1605 **George Weymouth** explores the Maine coast for the English, investigating the Kennebec and St. George's Rivers.

1606 **King James I** splits England's New World claims into Northern and Southern Virginia, which are soon to be separated by the Dutch colony of New Netherlands. Northern Virginia, which would come to be called New England, extended from the eastern end of Long Island to the northern tip of Nova Scotia.

Maine's **Mount Desert Isle** is named by Samuel de Champlain, who observed that the summits of its rocky hills were without trees.

1607 Settlements are sent to both Virginias. Jamestown Colony was founded in the south. In the north, 120 adventurers attempted the **Sagadahoc Colony at Popham Beach, Maine**, near the mouth of the Kennebec River. The colonists built a small ship, the *Virginia*, the first vessel made in America by the English. A severe winter, a fire in the storehouse, and violent conflicts with the Indians prompted the survivors to return to England in 1608.

1608 Samuel de Champlain travels up the St. Lawrence River to **Quebec** and establishes the first permanent French colony in America. The next year he sailed to Lake Champlain and explored Vermont.

1609 In July **Henry Hudson** spends a week in Maine's Penobscot Bay. The next month, his ship *Half Moon* touched Cape Cod, and in October he sailed to the future site of Albany, New York, on the river that bears his name. Because Hudson's explorations were sponsored by the Netherlands, the Hudson River Valley was claimed and colonized by the Dutch.

1612 **Anne Bradstreet**, destined to become America's first notable poet, is born Anne Dudley in England. She moved to America with her husband in 1630.

1614 **John Smith** explores New England and makes the best map to date of the coast from Penobscot Bay to Cape Cod, giving New England, Plymouth, Cape Ann, and the Charles River their English names. A second vessel on this expedition was commanded by Thomas Hunt, who kidnapped twenty native men at Plymouth and seven more at Cape Cod, and sold them as slaves in Spain. One of those enslaved was named **Squanto**, who traveled from Spain to England and eventually to Newfoundland where, in 1618, he met Thomas Dermer who was on his way to trade in Massachusetts. Dermer took Squanto with him.

The history of the **Connecticut River** begins when Adriaen Block, a Dutch explorer, enters a river the natives call "Quaneh-ta-cut," claims the land around it, and trades with the Indians who bring furs down the river in bark canoes. Block and his company had lost their first ship to fire and had spent the winter on Manhattan Island building a new one, which they named the *Restless*.

1616-17　An **epidemic** destroys many of New England's native Americans. Between Saco Bay in Maine and Narragansett Bay in Rhode Island, the population of native coastal peoples was reduced from 100,000 in 1617 to 5,000 by 1619. The disease is suspected to have been a European childhood illness such as chicken pox or measles. English settlers will think that Divine Providence had removed the biggest obstacle to New England's settlement and had left cleared fields for their convenience.

1620　The *Mayflower* sails from England, landing at Provincetown in November, and moving on to Plymouth in late December. Of the 102 passengers on the *Mayflower*, 41 were Separatists, and only 27 of these were adults; the other 61 Pilgrims came to Plymouth for secular reasons. Their winter diet and shelter were inadequate; only fifty Pilgrims survived until spring.

1621　The **Pilgrims** are pleasantly surprised to meet a bilingual Wampanoag named Squanto (see 1614). With Squanto as translator, discussions were held between the English leaders and Massasoit, the Wampanoag sachem, and peace was secured. Plymouth Colony's successful coexistence with the Wampanoags persuaded Puritans organizing in England that Massachusetts Bay was a feasible site for their colony.

1623　New Hampshire's first white settlement is a trading and fishing village established by David Thomson near the mouth of the Piscataqua River. By 1630 the principal settlement here was called **Strawbery Banke**, which in 1653 became Portsmouth.

English settlement at **Gloucester, Massachusetts** begins with a fishing colony sponsored by the Dorchester Company.

Kittery, Maine, is settled this year. In 1647 Kittery became the first Maine town to incorporate.

1624 **William Blackstone** and others disembark at Plymouth. Blackstone (also spelled Blaxton) took up residence on the side of a hill on a peninsula at the mouth of the Charles River, becoming the first Englishman to live on Beacon Hill. In 1631 Blackstone sold his holdings to the Puritans and moved to the river that is named after him, thus becoming the first white occupant of present-day Rhode Island. The orchard he planted bore fruit for several centuries. Blackstone died in 1675 a few days before the beginning of King Philip's War. One of the tales told of him is that when he was too old to travel on foot, Blackstone rode upon a bull he had trained for the purpose.

Plymouth Colony establishes trading posts at the future site of **Augusta, Maine**.

1626 The Gloucester colonists move to **Salem** to take up better farmland.

Puritan leaders in England form the **Massachusetts Bay Company** and are chartered to form a colony north of Plymouth.

1628 Autocratic **John Endicott** is sent to govern Salem. The original settlers soon moved to Beverly.

1629 **Maine** and **New Hampshire** begin to take form with the division of the large tract of northern lands that had been granted to proprietors Fernando Gorges and John Mason. Maine went to Gorges, and Mason received land between the Merrimack and Piscataqua Rivers, which he called New Hampshire after his native English county.

The **Massachusetts Bay Colony** is chartered and granted all of the land from three miles south of the Charles River to three miles north of the Merrimack River, and west to the "South Sea," as the Pacific Ocean was then named. Six ships delivered 406 people to Salem. Some of these moved on to establish Charlestown at the mouth of the Charles River.

1630 **Boston** is founded. John Winthrop, governor of the Massachusetts Bay Colony, landed at Salem but disliked it and went to Charlestown. Because Charlestown lacked a suitable water supply, Winthrop accepted William Blackstone's invitation to join him on the Shawmut Peninsula where there were good springs. The town established on Shawmut Peninsula was at first called Trimountain, but it was soon renamed Boston.

John Winthrop

When he sailed for the New World, Winthrop carried with him the charter of the Massachusetts Bay Colony, which was an indication that the administrative center of the new colony was to be in America, not in England.

Fifteen hundred **Puritans** immigrated to Massachusetts this year, more than doubling the English population of New England. By the end of September five new towns have begun: Watertown, Roxbury, Dorchester, Medford, and Saugus.

John Eliot arrived in Boston from England and became minister at the church at Roxbury. The following year he married Ann Mumford.

1632 Edward Winslow visits the **Connecticut River**. Massachusetts Bay colonists began to think of expanding in that direction.

1633 The Dutch build a fort, the House of Hope, on the Connecticut River at the site of present-day **Hartford, Connecticut**. When Massachusetts Puritans sailed past the fort's cannons to settle at **Windsor**, the Dutch held their fire. Others from Massachusetts began the town of **Wethersfield** on land they purchased from the sachem Sowheag. John Oldham and three others traveled overland from Watertown, Massachusetts, to the Connecticut River.

Gristmills powered by water were in operation in Massachusetts at Boston, Roxbury, and Saugus.

Cambridge, Massachusetts, was protected by a log palisade a mile and a half long.

1634 Voters from each Bay Colony town choose three representatives to the **Massachusetts General Court**, but voting is restricted to members of the Congregational church.

Roger Williams returns from England with Rhode Island's charter in 1644.

1635 **Roger Williams**, the minister at Salem, expresses his belief in religious freedom, and states that the English king cannot give away land owned and occupied by Indians. Williams was removed from his position and was to be sent back to England, but he fled to Narragansett Bay and spent the winter with Massasoit and the Wampanoags.

William Pynchon of Roxbury follows the Bay Path west until he reaches the Connecticut River at Agawam, where he founds a new town. In 1639 Agawam decided that it was part of Massachusetts and changed its name to Springfield.

1636 **Providence Plantation** is founded by Roger Williams and five companions on land purchased from the Narragansett Indians. The following year Williams helped **Anne Hutchinson** and her followers buy Aquidneck Island from the sachems Canonicus and Miantinomi. Like Williams, Hutchinson had been expelled from Massachusetts for expressing dissident religious views. On Aquidneck—soon to be known as Rhode Island—the town of Portsmouth was settled in 1637, and **Newport** in 1638. There were many **wolves** on the island, and arrangements were made with Miantinomi to have them hunted down. Despite the efforts of the Narragansetts, a decade later the English were still trying to rid Rhode Island of wolves.

Harvard College is founded in Cambridge, Massachusetts.

Proprietor **Fernando Gorges** establishes Maine's first government.

Thomas Hooker leads 100 followers from Cambridge to the Connecticut River, where they created **Hartford** on land deeded by the sachem Sequasson. At first it was called New Town, but soon it was named after Hertford, England, the home town of several important pioneers.

Connecticut Colony is formed by the towns of Hartford, Wethersfield, and Windsor.

1637 The **Pequot War** follows years of tension and several violent episodes. English from Connecticut, Massachusetts, and Plymouth, aided by Mohegans and Narragansetts, made a surprise attack on the Pequot town at Mystic. By setting fire to the houses and shooting those who fled the flames, they slaughtered 700 people in less than an hour. The surviving

Pequots attempted to withdraw to the Hudson River to join the Mohawks, but they were pursued and most were captured or killed. The Pequot leader, Sassacus, succeeded in reaching the Mohawks, only to be put to death by the people he hoped would protect him.

1638 **New Haven Colony** is founded by Massachusetts Puritans at a place on Long Island Sound called Quinnipiac by the natives. A large tract was bought from the sachem Momaguin for twelve cloth coats, twelve brass spoons, twelve hatchets, twenty-four knives, twelve porringers, and four cases of French knives and scissors.

The first Baptist church in America is founded by **Roger Williams** at Providence.

1639 The **Fundamental Orders of Connecticut** constitute organized government in that colony. Adopted at Hartford in January, the Fundamental Orders gave citizenship to all who were accepted residents of their towns—they did not have to belong to the church, as they did in Massachusetts. The first governor of the colony was **John Haynes**. One of the first actions of the colonial government was to standardize the size of bricks. The original towns of Connecticut Colony were Windsor, Wethersfield, and Hartford—the settlements at New Haven, Milford, and Guilford were independent.

1640 The **Great Migration of Puritans** took place in the decade between 1630 and 1640. Twenty thousand immigrants came to New England before Puritans under Oliver Cromwell took over the government of England, eliminating their need for a safe haven. In the ensuing civil war Charles I was arrested and was executed in 1649.

The *Bay Psalm Book*, the **first book printed in America**, is published in Cambridge by Stephen Daye.

Whitefield House, 1640

Whitefield House is built in Guilford. It is Connecticut's oldest house, and is thought to be the oldest stone house in New England.

1641 The colony of **New Hampshire unites with Massachusetts**. It remained part of the Bay Colony until 1679.

New Haven Colony sets up a free school.

1642 Massachusetts requires **parents to teach their children to read**. After 1647 every Massachusetts town with more than fifty families was required to employ a schoolmaster to teach reading and writing.

Mount Washington, the highest of New Hampshire's White Mountains, is climbed by Darby Field. Indians guided Field to within eight miles of the summit but stopped there because they believed that they would die if they went to the mountain's top. Field found glistening stones on Mount Washington that he thought were diamonds; they turned out to be quartz crystals.

1643 The **United Colonies of New England**, a confederation of Plymouth, Massachusetts, Connecticut, and New Haven, is established to unite English interests in opposition to their Dutch neighbors in New Netherlands. After New Netherlands became New York in 1664, the United Colonies had no more meetings.

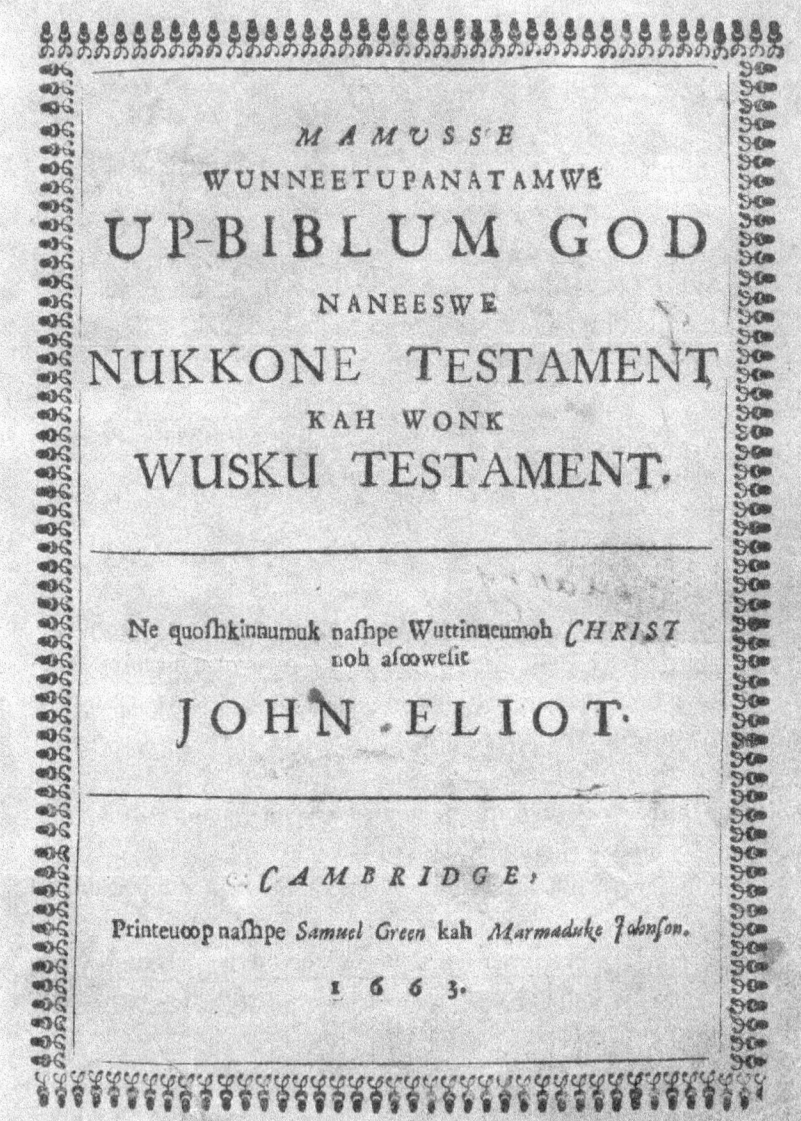

Title page, Eliot Bible

1644 **Rhode Island** is chartered as a self-ruling colony with **freedom of worship**. In 1647, the independent colonies around Narragansett Bay united under a charter that Roger Williams obtained in England. Connecticut and Massachusetts considered Rhode Island an aggregation of heretics, ignored it, and refused to trade with it, so Rhode Island formed an economic relationship with the Dutch in New Netherlands.

1645 **Roxbury Latin School** is founded in Roxbury, Massachusetts.

The Bay Colony has twenty-three churches. Attendance and financial support were compulsory. Although Puritan doctrine softened during the second half of the century, Massachusetts and Connecticut were slow to separate church from state.

1646 **John Eliot** begins preaching to the Massachusetts Indians in their own tongue. Natick, the first and most enduring of the Indian towns Eliot founded, was established in 1651. A decade later, Eliot's translation of the Bible was published, using a version of written Algonquian that he devised. By 1674, with the aid of funds raised in England, Eliot and his white and Indian colleagues had created fourteen towns of "praying Indians" throughout central Massachusetts.

Saugus Ironworks is built under the guidance of Richard Leader. The initiator and financial organizer of the enterprise was John Winthrop Jr., well-educated son of the Massachusetts governor. After being refined from ore found in bogs, iron was made into bars of stock for use by blacksmiths and was cast into kettles and firebacks (tablets of iron set at the back of fireplaces to reflect heat into the room).

1647 Rhode Island organizes its first government, officially named the "Incorporation of Providence Plantations in the Narraganset Bay in New England."

Heavy use of **tobacco** in Connecticut inspires a law stipulating that "no one under twenty years nor any other that hath not allreaddy accustomed himself to the Use thereof should take any Tobacco until he had a Certifcat from someone approved in Physicke that it is usefull for him."

1648 **Corporal punishment** is common in New England colonies, even for minor offenses. A Connecticut court ruled as follows:

> The Court adjudgeth Peter Bussaker for his filthy and profane expressions (namely, that he hoped to meete some of the members of the church in hell ere long, and he did not but question that he should) to be committed to prison, there to be kept in safe custody, till the sermon, and then to stand the time thereof in the pillory, and after the sermon to be severely whipped.

1649 Wethersfield, Connecticut, builds its first ship. **Shipbuilding** became an important industry in this town.

1650 **Anne Bradstreet** becomes America's first recognized poet when her *Tenth Muse* is published in London. Simon Bradstreet, her husband, will become the governor of Massachusetts Bay Colony. Anne lived in North Andover, Massachusetts, until her death in 1672. A sample stanza from her poem entitled "Contemplations":

> When I behold the heavens as in their prime,
> And then the earth (though old) stil clad in green,
> The stones and trees, insensible of time,
> Nor age nor wrinkle on their front are seen;
> If winter come, and greeness then do fade,
> A Spring returns, and they more youthful made;
> But Man grows old, lies down, remains where once he's laid.

1652 **Pine tree shillings** are made from Spanish dollars and other sources of metal at a Massachusetts mint operated by John Hull. Because the colonies were not permitted to manufacture money (minting was a royal prerogative), the shillings, although coined continuously until 1686, were all dated 1652 to give the impression that the minting ceased the year it began, at a time when the English throne was vacant.

1654 The Dutch are expelled from their fort at Hartford after decades of being crowded and insulted by their English neighbors.

1658 The first Jews arrive in Newport, Rhode Island, taking advantage of its religious toleration, as did many Quakers. The business activities of these two groups contributed to Newport's rise as a commercial center.

On Cape Cod a Quaker meeting is established in the town of Sandwich. Due to persecution, its members helped form a new settlement, in 1660, at Suckanesset, which became **Falmouth** in 1694.

1659 **Quakers are hanged** in Boston. Mary Dyer was condemned to die with William Robinson and Marmaduke Stevenson, but Dyer was reprieved at the last minute and sent to Rhode Island. She returned the following spring and this time her execution was carried out. In 1660 the British monarchy was restored and the Puritans' persecution of Quakers was halted by Charles II, who sent a Quaker as his emissary to the Massachusetts governor.

This statue of Mary Dyer, by Sylvia Shaw Judson, is next to the Massachusetts State House in Boston.

1660　The "regicide" judges (those who had signed the death-warrant of Charles I) arrive in Boston. Soon after the coronation of Charles II they fled to New Haven and Milford, Connecticut, and went into hiding. In 1664 they went to Hadley, Massachusetts, where the minister kept two of them hidden in his house for many years.

Celebration of Christmas was forbidden by law in Massachusetts but New England Puritanism did not frown on **alcohol**. Cider and beer were served with every meal including breakfast, and both men and women used tobacco.

1661　**Massasoit dies** and his son Metacomet, called Philip by the English, becomes sachem of the Wampanoag.

Connecticut's General Court begins meeting in Hartford in the upper room of Jeremy Adams's tavern, which served as the legislative chamber for half a century. (Money was voted to build a state house in 1719.) The General Court decided to acknowledge allegiance to Charles II and to send John Winthrop, Jr. to attempt to obtain a colonial charter.

1662　Winthrop succeeds in obtaining a **charter for Connecticut Colony**, giving it land seventy-three miles wide from Narragansett Bay to the Pacific Ocean, bounds that include New Haven and Rhode Island. New Haven Colony had little desire to join Connecticut but because the prospect of being swept into New York was clearly the greater evil, New Haven merged with Connecticut in December of 1664.

At Portsmouth, New Hampshire, a cage is constructed for the display of miscreants "such as sleep or take tobacco on the Lord's Day out of the meeting in the time of public service."

1663　Charles II grants **Rhode Island** a new charter that further clarifies the colony's policy of free thought: "no person within the colony, at any time hereafter shall be in any wise molested, punished, disquieted, or called in question for any difference of opinion in matters of religion."

1664 **New Netherland is seized** by England's Charles II, who sent four ships to force Dutch capitulation. Charles gave the area to his brother, the Duke of York. New Netherland and its principal town, New Amsterdam, were renamed **New York**. No effort was made to impose the English language or religion on the Dutch.

Settlement of present-day **Vermont** begins when the French erect a fort on Isle La Motte in Lake Champlain.

1672 **Roger Williams**, at age seventy-three, rows a boat all day to reach Newport from Providence because he is determined to join in a debate with some Quakers.

1674 Wearing silk and having long hair are the offenses for which thirty young Connecticut men are arrested this year.

1675 **King Philip's War** begins. The Wampanoag sachem leads an attempt to extinguish the Massachusetts Bay Colony. Hostilities commenced in July with Indian attacks on Swansea and Mendon. Though whites outnumbered the Indians, in the fall of 1675 the English were forced to face the possibility of their annihilation as the towns of Brookfield, Dartmouth, Deerfield, Groton, Lancaster, Mendon, Middleborough, Northfield, Simsbury, Warwick, Wickford, Worcester, and Wrentham were destroyed. The Great Swamp Fight took place in December when troops from the Puritan colonies invaded neutral Rhode Island to drive the Narragansetts from their homes.

1676 The Indians have the advantage during the winter and spring, but their efforts weaken as they deplete the supplies of the villages they have captured and their own towns and crops are burned by the whites. Most of Philip's warriors dispersed or surrendered during the summer, and Philip was killed in August.

Massachusetts and Plymouth lost 600 people—a tenth of the white male population—and fifty towns. The Indian losses were about 3000, approximately one-third of their population. Most Indian captives were executed or sold into slavery in the West Indies. Some of the surviving Indians fled to Maine and incited the local Abenakis to destroy white settlements at Casco, Pemaquid, Cape Neddick, Black Point, and Arrowsic.

Despite the fear and tension of war, there was romance on Cape Cod. A young woman named Hetty Shepard wrote in her diary:

> March 20. Sabbath at meeting. Mr. Willard spoke to the second commandment. Mr. Eliot prayed. While we were ceasing for half an hour, I saw Samuel Checkly and smiled; this was not the time to trifle and I repented, especially as he looked at me so many times after that I found my mind wandering from the psalm. And afterwards, when the Biskets, Beer, Cider, and Wine were distributed he whispered to me that he would rather serve me than the elders, which was a wicked thing to say, and I felt myself to blame.

Samuel Checkly and Hetty Shepard married the following year.

1679 **New Hampshire separates from Massachusetts** and is established as a royal colony, with Portsmouth as its capital.

Wild turkeys, plentiful when the English arrived in Massachusetts, were by this time becoming rare. Soon they were eliminated from the region, but were restored in the 1970s and had become ubiquitous by 2010.

1685 In an attempt to tighten control of the colonies, James II appoints **Sir Edmund Andros** governor of the newly organized "Dominion of New England." There was bitter opposition within the colonies because they had become accustomed to a large degree of self-rule.

Sir Edmund Andros

1686 **Andros arrives in Boston** in the frigate *Kingfisher*, with a guard of British soldiers, to be captain-general and governor-in-chief of New England.

The **Huguenots** are banished by Louis XIV. About 200,000 Protestants leave France, many of whom come to New England.

1687 According to Connecticut legend, Governor Andros demanded that the colony's charter be surrendered at a meeting in Hartford. At a signal, all of the candles were extinguished, and when they were relit, the charter was gone! It was hidden in the hollow of a large tree celebrated thereafter as the **Charter Oak**, which finally blew down in 1856. Andros took power anyway.

Connecticut's Charter Oak

1688 In **England's "Glorious Revolution,"** James II is deposed and William and Mary are enthroned.

The **Abenaki revolt** in Maine. Pemaquid was abandoned, and Dover, New Hampshire, was sacked.

1689 News of the "Glorious Revolution" reaches New England. **Colonists gleefully arrest Governor Andros** and put an end to the Dominion of New England.
Connecticut produced its charter from hiding and resumed its previous mode of government. One effect of the Dominion of New England was the permanent reduction of the power of the Puritan oligarchy.

The **French and Indian Wars** begin—a prolonged struggle between England and France. This conflict had four parts: King William's War, Queen Anne's War, King George's War, and the French and Indian War.

1690 Portland is destroyed by French and Indians. By the next year the only Maine towns still standing are Wells, Kittery, York and settlements on the Isles of Shoals.

1691 **Plymouth** is incorporated into the Massachusetts Bay Colony. The charter of their union provided for "liberty of conscience to all Christians, except Papists."
Massachusetts also absorbed **Maine**, having over the years purchased the holdings of its proprietors. Until it became a state in 1820, Maine remained part of Massachusetts.

1692 **Witch trials at Salem** result in the execution by hanging of fourteen women and five men. Another man died while authorities attempted to force a confession by having him "pressed" with stones.

1696 In giving Colonel Thomas Howe permission to keep an inn at Marlborough, Massachusetts, the town stipulates that "he shall not suffer to have any playing at cards, dice, tally, bowls, ninepins, billiards, or any other unlawful game or games in his said house . . . nor shall he entertain any persons of jolly conversation or given to tippling."

1697   During an Indian attack on Haverhill, Massachusetts, a woman named **Hannah Dustin** is taken prisoner. A few nights later, with the help of another woman and a young boy, Dustin killed ten of her captors as they slept, and made good her escape.

The **Peace of Ryswick** ends King William's War.

Salem witch trial judge **Samuel Sewall** publicly confesses his errors at Boston's South Church.

1698   Because numerous **pirates** are based in New England, the British government orders the colonial governments to repress them. Captain Kidd was arrested in Boston and sent to England, where he was executed in 1700.

Narragansett Pacer

1700s

The **Narragansett Pacer**, a breed of saddle horse, is developed on Rhode Island plantations.

1701 **Yale College** is founded. The first commencement was held at Saybrook, Connecticut, but in 1716 the college moved to New Haven. Originally called the Collegiate School, in 1718 it took the name of Elihu Yale, a New Haven native, governor of Britain's East India Company and principal benefactor of the college.

1702 **Queen Anne's War** begins. Abenaki and French attack English outposts in Maine.

1704 Deerfield, Massachusetts is attacked by French and Indians. John Williams and most of his large family were captured or killed. His seven-year-old daughter Eunice was taken to Canada, where she was raised as a Catholic and married an Iroquois. When she came home for a visit in 1740, she astonished her family by choosing to return to her life in Canada.

Sperm whale and whale boat

1712 The first **sperm whale** is brought to Nantucket and found to contain a large quantity of valuable oil that could be burned in lamps. Whaling ships seeking sperm whales began making longer voyages into deep water and by 1730 they were venturing to Brazil and to the Arctic.

1713 A peace treaty between Great Britain and France ends **Queen Anne's War** and inaugurates expansion into western and northern New England. Nova Scotia and Newfoundland became British colonies.

America's first **schooner** is built in Gloucester, Massachusetts.

1714 Fort Dummer, Vermont's first permanent white settlement, is built near present-day Brattleboro to protect Massachusetts's frontier.

1715-90

Most New England houses built in this period are **Georgian**, a style typified by symmetrical designs with the door in the center and windows evenly spaced on either side. Often there were tall, slender windows called *lights* beside the doors. Georgian house styles remained popular well into the 1800s.

1716 A house is built in Sudbury, Massachusetts, that will become famous as the setting of Longfellow's *Tales of a Wayside Inn* (see 1807).

Wigs have become very fashionable in New England despite the objections of Puritan preachers.

North America's first lighthouse is built in Boston Harbor on Little Brewster Island.

1719 **Scotch-Irish immigrants** settle in Londonderry, New Hampshire, where they introduced the manufacture of linen and the cultivation of potatoes.

April Fool's Day is scorned by Boston's Judge Samuel Sewall, who wrote in his diary:

> April 1. In the morning I dehorted Sam Hirst and Grindell Rawson from playing Idle tricks because 'twas the first of April: They were the greatest fools that did so. New England men came hither to avoid anniversary days, the keeping of them such as 25th of December.

Strict Congregationalists resisted the temptations of **Christmas** for many more years; it was not celebrated throughout New England until the time of the Civil War.

1721 New England suffers from a **smallpox epidemic**. Boston surgeon Zabdiel Boylston experimented with inoculation, but not until 1796 was there an effective vaccine. Boylston's innoculations were controversial but he received the support of influential minister Cotton Mather, who later wrote America's first medical treatise.

1722 **Billiards** can be played in a pub in Charlestown, Massachusetts.

1728 The *Boston News Letter* of November 18 prints its estimate of the daily expenses of food:

> Breakfast 1d. a Pint of Milk 2d 3d
> Dinner. Pudding Bread meat Roots Pickles Vinegar Salt and Cheese 9d
> (In this article of the Dinner I would include all the Rai-

sins Currants Suet Flour Eggs Cranberries Apples & where there are children all their Intermeal Eating)

Supper As the Breakfast 3d

Small Beer for the Whole Day 1 1/2d

For one Person a Day in all ....ls. 4 1/2d

Twelve pence (d) made a shilling (s), and twenty shillings made a pound.

1729 The **South Meeting House** is constructed in Boston. Phyllis Wheatley, America's first published African American poet, worshipped there.

1730 Boston's **Long Wharf** extends 2000 feet from State Street to deep water.

1732 **Iron ore** is discovered at Salisbury, Connecticut. In the ensuing decades several ironworks began operations in this area. Cannons were cast here for the American Revolution and to arm the *Constitution* and other warships.

1735 **Paul Revere** is born in Boston.

A religious revival called the **Great Awakening** is inspired by Jonathan Edwards of South Windsor, Connecticut, whose preaching emphasized a wrathful God and the punishment of sinners. Those who opposed this movement sought milder doctrines in independent "New Light" churches or joined the comparatively democratic Baptists. Baptist women voted on church affairs.

1741 The boundary between Massachusetts and New Hampshire is surveyed.

1744 Abigail Adams is born Abigail Smith in Weymouth, Massachusetts, the daughter of a Congregational minister.

King George's War begins, the third in the series of conflicts known collectively as the French and Indian Wars.

1745   The French fortress at Louisbourg on Cape Breton Island is attacked by English colonists. The action was instigated by William Vaughn of Damariscotta, Maine, and led by William Pepperell of Kittery. Positioned to control access to Canada, Louisbourg was the New World headquarters of the French Navy. The fortress was considered impregnable because it was protected on three sides by deep water and by a marsh on the fourth side.

The Yankees captured the guns of a small companion fort and, by heroic labors, build a causeway into the marsh. The guns were dragged onto the causeway and fired upon the city. Running low on supplies and suffering from the cannonade, Louisbourg capitulated, giving colonial New England its paramount military triumph. Pepperell was made a baronet by the British, who were quite surprised at the success of the untrained Yankees.

1748   The **Treaty of Aix-la-Chapelle** ends King George's War. A provision of the treaty returned Louisbourg to the French, which enraged New Englanders.

1749   America's third **lighthouse** is erected at Narragansett, Rhode Island.

1754   The **French and Indian War** begins. This war had important results: France lost its New World colonies, Britain accumulated debt, and American military leaders such as George Washington gained combat experience.

Joshua Moor dies and leaves his house in Lebanon, Connecticut, to Reverend Eleazer Wheelock, the town's pastor, who had been preaching to Native Americans since 1735. Wheelock gathered Delaware, Mohegan, and Mohawk students and formed Moor's Indian Charity School, which moved to Hanover, New Hampshire, in 1770 and eventually became **Dartmouth College**.

An almanac published in Connecticut by Roger Sherman included this prediction for December's weather: "Freezing cold weather, after which comes a storm of snow, but how long after I don't say."

1755   The French residents of Acadia, which the British call Nova Scotia, are expelled by the British. Some of the French moved to Louisiana, where their descendants would be known as **Cajuns**, derived from Acadians. Others dispersed throughout New England.

1756   **Paul Revere** serves briefly in the French and Indian War. Upon his return to Boston he married Sarah Orne and took up silversmithing, which had been his father's trade.

1759   **Rogers' Rangers** massacre of Native Americans at St. Francis, Quebec, secured northern New England for settlements from the British colonies.

1760-63

New Hampshire's Governor Benning Wentworth makes 138 land grants in present-day Vermont, which were subsequently known as the Hampshire Grants. The first town to be chartered was called **Bennington**.

1763   The **Treaty of Paris** ends the French and Indian Wars. It gave Britain control of all of Canada and all land east of the Mississippi River.

Moses Brown founds Rhode Island College. In 1770 the college moved to Providence, and in 1804 changed its name to **Brown**.

Newport's **Touro Synagogue** is dedicated this year. The oldest continuously operating synagogue building in North America, it was named after Judah Touro, a successful merchant who contributed funds for construction.

1764   Britain places **Vermont** under the control of New York by declaring the Connecticut River to be the boundary between New York and New Hampshire. New York attempted to expel settlers from New Hampshire who refused to re-purchase their land, thus initiating thirteen years of tension. The **Green Mountain Boys** formed in 1770 to defend what they regarded as their property rights. In 1774 the governor of New York offered a reward of fifty pounds apiece for the capture of leaders of the Green Mountain Boys.

Abigail Smith marries John Adams. John Quincy Adams, the second of their six children, will be the sixth president of the United States.

1765 Attempting to raise money to pay debts from the French and Indian War, Britain passes a **Stamp Act** requiring Americans to purchase stamps for legal and business papers, pamphlets, and newspapers.

Chocolate is first made in North America at a mill on the Neponset River in Massachusetts.

1766 In Providence, the **Daughters of Liberty** form to oppose the Stamp Act. To reduce imports from Britain, they spun wool at all-day meetings. The president and first graduating class of Rhode Island College all wore homespun clothing to commencement to underline their admiration of the Daughters of Liberty. Such colonial protests prompted repeal of the Stamp Act, but Britain continued attempts to tax the colonies.

1767 Parliament passes the **Townshend Acts**, which placed a tax on glass, paper, paints, and tea.

1768 **British troops are sent to Boston**, which had become a hotbed of resistance to the authority of the Mother Country. Throughout New England the schism between "Patriots" and "Loyalists" deepened.

Paul Revere placed this advertisement in the Boston Evening Post:
> Whereas many Persons are so unfortunate as to lose their Fore Teeth by Accident or Otherways to their

great Detriment not only in looks but in speaking both in public and private. This is to inform all such that they can have them replaced with Artificial Ones that look as well as the Natural and answer the End of Speaking by Paul Revere Goldsmith near the head of Dr. Clarkes wharf.

1769 The British ship *Liberty* is burned at a dock in Newport.

1770 The **Boston Massacre**. Under attack by a stone-throwing mob, British soldiers opened fire, killing five people. Even though they were tried in Boston, the soldiers, defended in court by John Adams, were found to have acted in self-defense. Nevertheless, Patriots generated propaganda from the incident. A Boston newspaper printed Paul Revere's engraving of the shooting of "unarmed" citizens. The British government canceled all of the Townshend Act taxes except for a small levy on tea.

1772 The **Gaspee Affair**. The *Gaspee* was a revenue cutter that had been quite successful in thwarting smuggling in Narragansett Bay until it ran aground near Providence, thus giving a mob of locals the chance to beat up the crew and burn their ship. British officials did not succeed in arresting the offenders, but their effort to do so deepened the rift between Britain and the American colonies and led to the establishment of **Committees of Correspondence**, which became an important channel of communication among the colonies.

1773 The **Boston Tea Party**. The night before three ships of British-owned tea were to be unloaded, Patriot leader Sam Adams held a public meeting at the Old South Meeting House. On Adams's cue, "This meeting can do nothing more to save the country," the Sons of Liberty went to the wharf and dumped 342 chests of tea into the harbor. One of the participants was Paul Revere.

1774 Parliament passes the **Intolerable Acts** (as they were known in America) in response to the Boston Tea Party. Britain closed the port of Boston and suspended the Massachusetts legislature, placing the colony under the rule of General Gage, who arrived in Boston with additional troops. The General's power was effective only within the city; the rest of the colony formed its own government. Companies of Patriot militia began training in towns throughout New England.

The colonies prepared for united action by holding a **Continental Congress**; John Adams represented Massachusetts.

In New Hampshire, Patriot activists called **Sons of Liberty** were warned by Paul Revere that British ships were coming to take military supplies stored at Fort William and Mary in Portsmouth Harbor. The colonists surprised the fort's small garrison and took ninety-nine kegs of gunpowder for use in the forthcoming war.

Patriots in York, Maine had their own tea party, but instead of dumping the tea into salt water, they burned it. The following spring another tea-burning took place in Providence.

Shaker leader Ann Lee arrives from England and begins converting Americans to her religious sect. Because Ann Lee was British and advocated pacifism, the Shakers encountered fierce resistance in their early years, but they persisted in advocating their celibate, communal way of life and by 1800 had established eleven communities in New York and New England with a combined population of 1,373. In the twentieth century Shaker numbers declined, and at present their only active community is at Sabbathday Lake in Maine.

1775 The American Revolution begins with the **Battle of Lexington and Concord**. British troops stationed in Boston under the command of General Gage were dispatched to seize Patriot munitions stored in Concord. Patriot leaders had anticipated this move, and companies of local militia called Minute Men had trained to meet such an emergency. When the British troop movement began on the night of April 18, a young Patriot from Boston, William Dawes, slipped by the British sentries and rode through Roxbury, Brookline, Cambridge, and Menotomy (Arlington) on his way to Lexington, spreading the alarm as he went.

"The Minute Man" by Daniel Chester French, 1875. Overlooking the site of the fight at Concord's bridge.

Two lanterns were hung in the steeple of Christ Church (now called Old North) to signal Patriots in Charlestown that the redcoats were moving by boat up the river rather than marching on Boston Neck. Meanwhile, Paul Revere was rowed across the mouth of the Charles River and lent a horse so that he could ride to Lexington. The bell in the Lexington meetinghouse called out the Minute Men. Revere was stopped by a British patrol, but Dr. Samuel Prescott carried the warning to Concord.

The British troops disembarked at East Cambridge in the early hours of April 19, and after a long delay began their march through what are now Somerville and Arlington. The column was confronted at dawn on Lexington Green by the town's Minute Men, under Captain John Parker, who ordered his seventy-seven men to "Stand your ground! Don't fire unless fired upon! But if they mean to have a war, let it begin here!"

The British commander, Major John Pitcairn, shouted to the Minute Men, "Lay down your arms, you damned rebels and disperse!" Seeing his men outnumbered ten to one, Captain Parker was willing to withdraw, but there was a gunshot—no one knows who fired it—and then a British volley killed eight Patriots.

The British continued to Concord and searched for arms, most of which had been hidden. A detachment was sent to the west of the village to guard the North Bridge over the Concord River. When Minute Men on the high ground across the river saw smoke from the village center, they believed that the British were setting fire to the town and they decided to force their way across the bridge. British guards fired from the bridge and the Minute Men returned fire. There were casualties on both sides, and the surviving British retreated to the center of town.

Patriot militia streamed toward Concord from all directions. By the time the scarlet-clad column began its withdrawal toward Boston, it was surrounded by hostile colonials. For the most part the Americans were held out of musket range of the column by British flankers, but where they could hold positions near the road they took a heavy toll. By the time they had reached Charlestown the British had lost 73 dead and 174 wounded. The Americans lost 49 dead and 40 wounded.

The British retreated into Boston and the Americans lay siege to the city.

George Washington took command of the Continental Army in Cambridge, in July of 1775. This statue stands in Boston's Public Garden.

In May, **Fort Ticonderoga** is captured by Vermont's Green Mountain Boys led by Ethan Allen and by Benedict Arnold. The following winter, fifty cannon from Ticonderoga were transported over the snow to Boston (see 1776).

The **Battle of Bunker Hill** takes place on June 17. Patriots had occupied high ground that threatened Boston, forcing the British to cross the Charles River to dislodge them. The Redcoats were eventually successful in capturing the hill, but they suffered fearful casualties in doing so, and the Americans' will to fight was demonstrated beyond doubt. To retaliate for sniper fire from the town, the British burned Charlestown.

Patriot forces are adopted by the Continental Congress. In July **George Washington** took command of the Continental Army in Cambridge.

Benedict Arnold leads American troops up the Kennebec River and across Maine to attempt the capture of Quebec. The attack was ill-conceived; the commanders had underestimated the difficulties of the journey. The force reached its destination in no condition to fight. Though reinforced by sea, Arnold was defeated.

In October, the **British navy destroys Falmouth** (now Portland, Maine) with warship guns. The British commander aimed his fire over the buildings until most residents had withdrawn. Tavernkeeper Alice Greely stayed with her establishment and put out fires as they started; hers was the only public building to survive.

1776 Fifty **cannons from Fort Ticonderoga** are moved over snow by draft animals and presented to General Washington in Cambridge. In March, Washington placed these guns on Dorchester Heights, from which they commanded Boston. The British were allowed to depart in safety with the proviso that they did not set fire to the town. Most of Boston's Loyalists left with the troops.

Abigail Adams wrote to her husband at Philadelphia:

> In the new Code of Laws which I suppose it will be necessary for you to make I desire you would **remember the Ladies**, and be more generous and favorable to them than your ancestors... If particular care and attention is not paid to the ladies we are determined to foment a rebellion, and will not hold ourselves bound by any laws in which we have no voice or representation.

Adams and the other forefathers disregarded this advice.

On the fourth of July the Declaration of Independence is proclaimed by the Continental Congress.

1777 New Hampshire troops win the **Battle of Bennington**, which was fought west of the town, in New York. The American commander at Bennington was General John Stark (1728-

1822), who had been a captive of the Abenaki for part of his youth, and from whom he had learned his wilderness skills. Speaking to his men before the battle, Stark said, "There are the redcoats, and they are ours, or this night Molly Stark sleeps a widow." Stark Peaks and the town of Stark, New Hampshire, bear the General's name. The Battle of Bennington led to the important American victory at Saratoga.

Vermont declares itself an independent republic and establishes its own coins and units of weight and measure.

Abigail Adams writes of wartime deprivations:

> There is a great scarcity of Sugar and coffee, articles which the female part of the State is very loath to give up, especially whilst they consider the great scarcity occasioned by the merchants having secreted a large quantity...It was rumored that an eminent stingy wealthy merchant (who is a bachelor) had a hogshead of coffee in his store which he refused to sell the committee under six shillings per pound. A number of females, some say a hundred, some say more, assembled with a cart and trunks, marched down to the warehouse and demanded the keys which he refused to deliver. Upon which one of them seized him by his neck and tossed him into the cart. Upon his finding no quarter he delivered the keys when they tipped up the cart and discharged him; then opened the warehouse, hoisted out the coffee themselves, put [it] into the trunks and drove off...A large concourse of men stood amazed, silent spectators of the whole transaction.

The sloop-of-war *Ranger* is launched at Kittery, Maine, and placed under command of John Paul Jones. *Ranger* hurried to France with word of the American victory at Saratoga, which helpd persuade France to support the cause of American independence.

1778   Phillips Academy is established in Andover, Massachusetts. Another Phillips Academy opened three years later in Exeter, New Hampshire.

1779   The **Penobscot Expedition**, an attempt to recapture territory in Maine held by the British, ends in failure. Paul Revere's conduct as commander of artillery was called into question.

1780   **Massachusetts adopts a constitution** written by John Adams. Its bicameral legislature and system of three governmental branches with countervailing powers was largely imitated in the federal constitution written eight years later.

May 19 was a phenomenally **dark day** in New England. Candles were in use at midday, and chickens went to roost. Heavy smoke from western forest fires is thought to have been the cause.

1780-86   Land between the Appalachians and the Mississipi had been claimed by Connecticut and Massachusetts in accordance with the terms of their colonial charters. During these years the claims were surrendered, but Connecticut retained its "Western Reserve," most of which was sold to benefit public education in the state.

1781   **Shaker founder Ann Lee** and several followers come to Massachusetts and start a Shaker community in the town of Harvard.

1783   **Noah Webster** of West Hartford, Connecticut, publishes his first spelling book, *A Grammatical Institute of the English Language*, spawning a craze for spelling bees, which become a popular recreation in much of New England. Webster's *American Dictionary of the English Language* appeared in 1828, the product of twenty-six years of labor. Webster's books on spelling and grammar sold so well that he is credited with giving America a uniform language.

Boston's **Old South Meeting House** installs a stove. The Evening Post printed this lament:

> Extinct the sacred fire of love,
> Our zeal grown cold and dead,
> In the house of God we fix a stove
> To warm us in their stead.

Whether or not to heat churches became a controversial issue in congregations throughout New England.

1784 Hartford and New Haven are incorporated as cities.

The *Empress of China* makes the first direct voyage of an American ship to Canton, returning with tea, silk, porcelain, and spices. Sales of this cargo were so profitable that New England ship owners rushed to enter the **China trade**. Maine ships that joined in this long-distance commerce include the *Red Jacket*, the *Water Witch*, the *Flying Dragon*, and the *Black Squall*. Salem, Massachusetts, was the home port for many ships engaged in the China trade. Profits accrued in this commerce were the original source of the wealth of some of New England's most prominent families.

1785 The *Falmouth Gazette*, Maine's first newspaper, is established to promote separation from Massachusetts.

America's first marble quarry is opened in Dorset, Vermont.

1786 The Humane Society of Massachusetts is founded to aid shipwrecked mariners. This group inspired the formation of the United States Life-Saving Service, which merged in 1915 with the Revenue Cutter Service to form the **U. S. Coast Guard**.

1787 **Shays' Rebellion** increases support for a stronger federal government. In the so-called rebellion, Daniel Shays led 1000 farmers in an attempt to capture the courthouse and arsenal at Springfield, Massachusetts, hoping to halt lawsuits for debt and to protest high land taxes. The farmers were routed by militia, but their desperate action succeeded in drawing attention to their plight.

1788   The new **United States Constitution** is ratified by Connecticut, Massachusetts, and New Hampshire. New Hampshire's ratification was the ninth and therefore caused the constitution to take effect. In the ensuing election, George Washington was elected president.

1790   **Rhode Island** finally ratifies the new Constitution.

Samuel Slater builds America's **first water-powered cotton spinning mill** on the Blackstone River in Pawtucket, Rhode Island, in partnership with Moses Brown. The machine-made thread was distributed to households in the area for weaving. Considered the beginning of the industrial revolution in America, the mills brought Slater fame and great wealth; at his death in 1835 he was worth $1,200,000.

1790-1850

The **whaling** industry is important not only to Nantucket, but also to Newport, Providence, and Warren, Rhode Island, and New Bedford, Massachusetts. At first, whaling ships stayed in New England waters but by about 1820 it was normal for whaling voyages to last three years and to circumnavigate the globe. A popular route took ships from New England ports to the Azores and the Cape Verde Islands, then around the Cape of Good Hope to the Bay of Whales in New Zealand. Whalers often called at the Hawaiian Islands for rest and recreation—the behavior of their crews was notorious—before sailing to the Bering Sea, then returning home by way of Cape Horn.

1791   Vermont joins the United States, the first state to enter after the original thirteen colonies. New York's land claims were setted by a payment of $30,000.

Salem has seven distilleries producing rum from molasses.

Portland Head Light is built, destined to become the oldest, most painted, and most photographed light house in America.

Portland Head Light

1792 Robert Bailey Thomas (1766-1846) publishes the first **Farmer's Almanack**. Thomas, a bookseller, schoolteacher, and amateur astronomer, published fifty-three more editions from Sterling, Massachusetts (present-day West Boylston) before his death in 1846. The title became *Old Farmer's Almanac* in 1848; publication continued without interruption for two centuries.

1793 **Eli Whitney** invents the cotton gin, making cotton much less expensive to produce. Abundant cotton grown in the South and improving technology gave rise to cotton mills throughout New England and created Northern interests favorable to slavery.

1794 Inexpensive jewelry becomes an important product of Providence after metal coating methods devised by Nehemiah Dodge led to large-scale manufacturing.

      The first **fire insurance** policy is written in Hartford, leading to the formation of the Hartford and New Haven Insurance

Company, the forerunner of the huge insurance industry that grew in Hartford during the nineteenth century.

Samuel Morey of Fairlee, Vermont, operates a **steamboat** on the Connecticut River fourteen years before Fulton's demonstration of the *Clermont*. John Fitch had steamed on the Delaware River in 1787.

The manufacture of **pottery** begins at Bennington, Vermont.

The **Springfield Armory**, the first federally-owned arms manufacturing facility, is established at Springfield, Massachusetts. Production of flintlock muskets began the following year, and the operation was continuous until 1968. The armory played a lead role in developing the "American System" of manufacturing, which relied on division of labor and increased use of machinery. The M-1 rifle, the basic infantry weapon of United States forces in World War II and Korea, was developed and produced at the Springfield Armory. The armory is now a museum with one of the world's largest collections of weapons.

Bowdoin College, Maine's oldest institution of higher learning, is founded. Nathaniel Hawthorne, Franklin Pierce, and Henry Wadsworth Longfellow will be alumni.

Sylvester Graham is born in Suffield, Connecticut. Graham played an important part in the vegetarian aspect of the reform movement of the 1830s and 1840s and published *Graham Lectures on the Science of Human Life and Bread and Bread-making*. His name became a commonplace because of his whole-grain crackers.

1796 **Connecticut's Old State House**, designed by Charles Bulfinch, is completed this year. The present Connecticut state house was built in 1880.

1797 The oak-hulled frigate *Constitution*, 204 feet in length, is launched on October 21 at Boston's shipyard. Paul Revere rolled the copper sheeting that armored the sides of the *Constitution*.

John Adams took office as the second President of the United States, with **Abigail Adams** as his First Lady.

1798 **Eli Whitney** establishes a firearms factory at Hamden, Connecticut. This was one of the first efforts to use the principle of interchangeable parts in manufacturing.

1799 The **Peabody Museum** is established in Salem by sea captains seeking a suitable repository for items they have collected during their voyages.

The Peirce Mansion is built in Portsmouth, New Hampshire, a classic example of **Federal architecture**, and one used as a model for many later houses. The centered front door was topped by a fanlight. Architect Charles Bulfinch was an apostle of this style during part of his career—Connecticut's Old State House was a Federal design.

1800s

1802 **Dorothea Dix**, one of the leading humanitarians of her age, is born in Hampden, Maine. She became an effective proponent of reform for asylums and prisons and was the chief of Union nurses during the Civil War.

America's first **Merino sheep** are imported from Spain. By 1840 Vermont and New Hampshire had two million Merinos, which had heavier wool than the breeds previously in use by American farmers.

1803 The *Constitution* participates in the successful effort to suppress the piracy of the Barbary powers in the Mediterranean Sea. Commodore Edward Preble, of Falmouth (Portland), Maine, commanded a fleet of seven ships sent to Tripoli.

The **Middlesex Canal**, one of the first public works projects in the United States, opens water transportation between the Merrimack River and Boston, running twenty-seven miles through seven towns. The canal made trade between Boston and New Hampshire more direct. The Boston & Lowell Railroad, built in 1835, served much the same purpose and operated all year (the canal froze during winter), causing the Middlesex Canal to cease operations in the 1840s.

Ralph Waldo Emerson is born on May 25, in Boston.

1804 A Vermont judge rules that **the only proof of ownership of a slave** is a "bill of sale from Almighty God."

Nathaniel Hawthorne, who will become famous as the author of *The Scarlet Letter* and *The House of the Seven Gables*, is born in Salem, Massachusetts. After an interlude at Brook Farm, (see 1841) Hawthorne married Sophia Peabody. The first three years of their marriage were spent at the Old Manse in Concord, Massachusetts.

1806 The **Boston and Hartford Turnpike** is built.

1807 In an attempt to avoid conflict with Britain, Congress passes the **Embargo Act**, which ruined American shipping but stimulated manufacturing. New England was badly hurt by the Embargo Act, and the following satirical verse was published in protest of the law.

> Our ships all in motion
> Once whiten'd the ocean
> They sail'd and return'd with their cargo;
> Now doom'd to decay
> They have fallen a prey
> To Jefferson, Worms, and Embargo.

The embargo was soon replaced with measures less drastic.

Poet **Henry Wadsworth Longfellow** is born in Portland, Maine. In his adult years he lived in Cambridge in the house that had been General Washington's headquarters. One of Longfellow's best known works is *Tales of a Wayside Inn* in which the Red Horse Inn of Sudbury, Massachusetts, was the setting for a series of tales. Here is Longfellow's description of the inn:

> A region of repose it seems,
> A place of slumber and of dreams,
> Remote among the wooded hills!
> For there no noisy railway speeds,
> Its torch-race scattering smoke and gleeds;
> But noon and night, the panting teams
> Stop under the great oaks, that throw
> Tangles of light and shade below,
> On roofs and doors and window sills.
> Across the road the barns display
> Their lines of stalls, their mows of hay,
> Through the wide doors the breezes blow,
> The wattled cocks strut to and fro,
> And, half effaced by rain and shine,
> The Red Horse prances on the sign.

1808 **Concord** becomes the capital of New Hampshire.

1810 **Cigar manufacture** begins in the valley of the Connecticut River. Cigar-making had previously been a cottage industry, a part-time occupation of farm wives. Connecticut Valley Broadleaf tobacco was favored for the outer wrapping of cigars, and demand for it is high until the 1920s, when cigarettes captured much of tobacco market.

The first bridge across the Connecticut River at Hartford opens to the public.

1812 The **War of 1812** begins. New England dissented because its economy was based on shipping, which was halted by the war. Before the war ended New England's political leaders briefly considered seceding from the union.
   The frigate *Constitution* defeats the British *Guerriere* in a naval battle off Nova Scotia in August. The *Constitution*, commanded by Isaac Hull, gained the nickname "Old Ironsides" in this battle because it withstood the enemy's cannon balls so well.

1813 In waters off Maine's Monhegan Island, the British brig *Boxer* fights the U.S.S. *Enterprise*. The *Boxer* was under Captain Blythe, twenty-eight years of age. The American commander, Lieutenant William Burrows, was a year younger. The two vessels were evenly matched. After hours of jockeying for position, firing began.
   Blythe died in the first minutes of the battle, and soon Burrows received a mortal wound, although he lived to accept the surrender of the *Boxer*. The *Enterprise* towed the British ship into Portland Harbor. The whole city turned out for the funeral of the two commanders, and they were buried side by side.

1814 A new kind of **textile mill** is built on the Charles River at Waltham, Massachusetts, by Francis Cabot Lowell and the Boston Manufacturing Company, which raised capital through a new and controversial method—the sale of stock. The mill, based on British designs, was the first in America to perform all of the operations necessary for converting raw cotton into finished cloth. The company's labor force consisted largely of young women recruited from farms. Success at Waltham prompted expansion on the Merrimack River and the creation of the city of Lowell. An average mill family in the early 1800s made about $650 a year, while the same family living on a farm made about $180 a year—but raised most of its own food.

Abigail and John Adams celebrate their golden wedding anniversary.

The **War of 1812 ends** with the Treaty of Ghent.

1815 The **Handel and Haydn Society** is started in Boston.

1816 New England's **Year without Summer**, also known as the Poverty Year, the Cold Year, and Eighteen hundred-and-froze-to-death. In the Connecticut Valley there was a heavy frost every month, with snow in June and drought for the rest of the growing season. The failure of crops encouraged "Ohio Fever" for migration to western lands. The cause is thought to have been the eruption of a volcano, Mount Tambora, on the island of Sumbawa, Indonesia.

Maine attempts to secede from the Commonwealth of Massachusetts, but the United States Constitution forbade the division of a state.

1817 **Henry David Thoreau**, naturalist and author of *Walden*, is born in Concord, Massachusetts.

Ralph Waldo Emerson enters Harvard College. He waited on tables during the college year and taught in secondary schools during the summer. Emerson was an early mentor of Thoreau's and gave the eulogy at his funeral (see 1862).

1818 **Paul Revere** dies at age eighty-three. **Abigail Adams** dies at seventy-four.

1819 Maine votes in favor of statehood.

The principles of **Unitarianism** are set forth by William Ellery Channing, a liberal Boston minister.

1820 The **Missouri Compromise** gives Maine independence from Massachusetts, and Maine enters the Union as the twenty-third state. In order to maintain the balance in the Senate, Maine was brought in as a free state so that Missouri could be allowed to enter as a slave state. Maine's first capital was Portland.

Coffee came into widespread use about this time, although it was derided by some as a dangerous drug.

1822 **Boston** is incorporated as a city.

Frederick Law Olmsted, environmentalist and landscape architect, is born in Hartford.

A public library opens in Dublin, New Hampshire, that has claims to being the **first free public library** in America, although Salisbury, Connecticut, had a free library for children in 1803.

1823 The **Champlain Canal** is constructed to allow boats to pass between Lake Champlain and the Hudson River.

Trinity College is established in Hartford by Episcopalians, as a theological alternative to Yale's Congregationalism. In its early years, Trinity was called Washington College.

Formal **teacher training** begins with a school opened for this purpose by Samuel Hall in Concord, Vermont.

1824 Poet, teacher, and editor **Lucy Larcom** is born in Beverly, Massachusetts. When Lucy was eleven, her father died, and the family moved to Lowell. Lucy went to work in the mill, but her education was not neglected.

At twenty-two she moved to Illinois where she taught school and continued her own studies. Larcom's *A New England Girlhood* was published in 1889. Here is the opening of her poem "By the Fireside:"

> What is it fades and flickers in the fire,
> Mutters and sighs, and yields reluctant breath,
> As if in the red embers some desire,
> Some word prophetic burned, defying death?

Lucy Larcom

The first known **strike** in an American factory takes places at a cotton mill in Pawtucket, Rhode Island, after the work day was made an hour longer and pay was cut by 25%. The workers succeeded in reversing the changes.

1825 The **Erie Canal** opens, connecting Lake Erie with the Hudson River. Cheap transportation of grain from the Ohio valley increased the difficulties facing New England farmers and gave New York an insurmountable commercial advantage over New England cities.

Along the **Blackstone River**, a canal is being built to connect Worcester with Providence.

The **ten hour workday** is the goal of striking Boston carpenters. Employers argued that so much leisure time would lead to dissipation and vice.

1800s

In Boston, **Quincy Market** is built, an example of the Greek Revival style popular in public buildings of this era.

1826 The **American Society for the Promotion of Temperance** is formed in Boston.

The manufacture of the **Concord Coach** begins in Concord, New Hampshire. This sturdy vehicle became a standard means of transportation on the western frontier.

Boston's **Union Oyster House** becomes a public eating place.

A **lyceum** is established at Millbury, Massachusetts, and within five years nearly every town has one of these lecture societies.

The **Granite Railway** is built in Quincy, Massachusetts, to move stone blocks for construction of the Bunker Hill Monument. The distance from the quarry to the water front was three miles. In order to secure a right-of-way, the Granite Railway Company was incorporated by the legislature in March. The first train ran on October 7—pulled by a horse. The Granite Railway operated for forty years without ever using steam power.

1827 **Swimming instruction** is offered in Boston.

1828 The **Farmington Canal** opens, allowing boats to pass between Southwick, Massachusetts, and New Haven, Connecticut. Ten years later the Hartford & New Haven Railroad deprived the canal of much of its business, though canal operations continued until 1845, when a drought delivered the final blow.

1830 Poet **Emily Dickinson** is born in Amherst, Massachusetts.

The first American steam-powered railroad is built in Baltimore.

The **USS *Constitution*** is condemned but Oliver Wendell Holmes writes, in "Old Ironsides,"

> Oh, better that her shattered hulk
> Should sink beneath the wave.

The ship was rebuilt and returned to service in 1833, used as a training ship, later as a barracks. In 1934 the *Constitution* became a memorial at the Boston Naval Shipyard. Presently docked at the Charlestown Navy Yard, the *Constitution* is the oldest warship afloat in the world.

USS Constitution *in 1997*

1830s Old Sturbridge Village recreates this decade of New England life at Sturbridge, Massachusetts.

1831 In Boston, William Lloyd Garrison begins publishing an antislavery newspaper he calls *The Liberator*.

1832 Augusta replaces Portland as the capital of Maine.

Harvard student Richard Henry Dana interrupts his studies to take a sea voyage for his health. He served as a hand on the brig *Pilgrim*, sailing around Cape Horn to California. Dana wrote of his experiences in *Two Years Before the Mast*.

1833 A Quaker named Prudence Crandall opens a school for "young ladies and little misses of color" in Canterbury, Connecticut. The legislature passed a statute forbidding schools for blacks. Before the question could be decided by litigation, a mob broke the school's windows, causing Crandall to give up and leave town. Fifty years later the state legislature voted her a pension.

1834 The Ursuline Convent in Charlestown, Massachusetts, is destroyed by an anti-Catholic mob.

An electric motor is built in Vermont by Thomas Davenport and patented three years later, but there was not yet a market for electric motors.

1835 The **Boston & Worcester Railroad** is completed, linking Massachusetts's two largest cities. In 1841, the Western Railroad pushed the connection west to the Hudson River at Albany. The Hartford & New Haven and the Boston & Lowell railroads also began operations in 1835, and New Hampshire's first railroad, the Nashua & Lowell, obtained a charter. It was only five miles long, from Nashua to the state line.

Harvard Medical School admits its first woman student.

1836 **Ralph Waldo Emerson publishes** *Nature*, written at the Old Manse in Concord, Massachusetts. About this time the so called "Transcendental Club" began its meetings. Bronson Alcott, George Ripley, Margaret Fuller, William Ellery Channing, Henry David Thoreau, and Elizabeth Peabody all participated in this loosely structured group. By promoting reform but defending individualism, the Transcendentalists helped America adjust to the industrial revolution. As steel, steam, and the telegraph changed the world, Emerson and his friends reminded their readers of non-material values.

The Bangor & Piscataquis, **Maine's first railroad**, connects Bangor with Old Town.

Winslow Homer is born in Boston. He became famous for paintings made near his home near Portland, Maine, at Prout's Neck, where in 1884 he built a studio overlooking the sea.

Mary Lyon founds **Mount Holyoke Female Seminary** at South Hadley, Massachusetts, which became Mount Holyoke College in 1888.

1837 Education reformer **Horace Mann** is given the leadership of the first Massachusetts State Board of Education. During the twelve years Mann held this post he achieved substantial progress in public education and teacher training.

1838 Putney, Vermont, is the site of a new religious community featuring "Bible Communism" or "**complex marriage**," in which non-monogamous sexual activity was permitted. Leader John Humphrey Noyes later established Oneida Community in New York on a similar basis.

1839 **Photography** comes to America. Francois Gouraud, a student of the French photography pioneer Louis Daguerre, arrived in the United States in the fall. The next year he trained several Bostonians to make daguerreotypes, and photography studios multiplied.

1800s

The "**Aroostook War**" results from a conflict about the boundary between Maine and Canada. Troops from New Brunswick and Maine faced each other across the St. John River until their commanders agreed that the river would be the border, and tension subsided. The boundary was officially fixed in 1842 by the Webster-Ashburton Treaty.

1840 Vermont has six times as many sheep as human beings. In the coming decades wool production in the West increased, and Vermont shifted toward dairy farming.

1840s Railroads expand rapidly across New England. In Connecticut, railroad mileage rose from 117 to 551 by the end of the decade. The New York & New Haven Railroad opened in 1848, making it possible to travel between Boston and New York by train.

1841 At **Brook Farm** in West Roxbury, Massachusetts, George and Sophia Ripley initiate an experimental community, and Adin Ballou starts the Hopedale Community at Milford. To explain the need for radical change, Ballou wrote:

> Even the more advanced classes in church and state, seeking the progress, the harmony, and happiness of mankind, propose little if anything more than the gradual improvement of society on the old basis of egoism, caste distinctions, competitive rivalry, shrewd and cunning practices, jealousy and hatred of race and nation.

In the 1840s at least sixty communities around the country searched for a form of group living that would improve society.

The whaler *Charles W. Morgan* is built at New Bedford, Massachusetts, for $23,000. A hundred years and thirty-seven voyages later she was brought to Mystic Seaport in Connecticut and placed on exhibit.

1842 Rhode Island adopts a new constitution, reorganizing representation in its General Assembly, which had become grossly unfair to urban areas. The change was prompted by the actions of Thomas Dorr and his followers who tried to capture the Providence Armory and set up a new Rhode Island government. Dorr was sentenced to life in prison, but was freed in 1845.

In a pioneering labor law, the work day for children in Massachusetts is limited to ten hours.

Fruitlands, Harvard, Massachusetts

1843 In June, Bronson Alcott and his followers and family move to a farm they call **Fruitlands** in the town of Harvard, Massachusetts, where they attempt to create a completely ethical community. Cotton clothing was rejected because cotton was raised by slaves. They did not use leather, because cattle had a right to keep their skins, nor wool, which they thought should be left upon the sheep. Eating meat was out, and although grains and other garden crops were permitted, they were suspect if the soil that grew them had been fertilized with manure or cultivated with the labor of animals. Alcoholic beverages, coffee, tea, and even milk were all scorned; their only drink was water. The Fruitlanders tried to wear only linen, the cloth made from flax, a crop already widely grown in Massachusetts. Seeking a food source cultivated by human labor, Alcott and his friends settled on fruit—thus, Fruitlands, though their farm had only a small orchard.

Preparations for the winter were entirely inadequate. The community diminished during the fall and perished by January.

Unlike the other Transcendentalist experiments, the duration of the Fruitlands venture was measured in months rather than years, but the memory of it is alive because its beautiful site and the original farmhouse are preserved by the Fruitlands Museums. One of Bronson Alcott's daughters, a willful little girl at the time of her stay at Fruitlands, was Louisa May Alcott, future author of *Little Women*.

Millerites expect the world to end this year in accordance with the prophecy of their leader, William Miller. Many of Miller's followers gave away their property in anticipation of the end.

1844 **Charles Goodyear** of New Haven, Connecticut, patents the vulcanization of rubber.

In Washington, D.C., Samuel Morse demonstrates the telegraph, which he had been working on since 1832.

1845 **Irish immigration** to Boston increases because of the potato famine. Penniless newcomers crowded into tenements in the North End, where they had a life expectancy of fourteen years.

Lowell, Massachusetts, savings banks hold $100,000 deposited by **mill girls** who work twelve to fourteen hours per day.

Henry David Thoreau lives at Walden Pond in Concord, Massachusetts, from July 4, 1845 until September 6, 1847. Thoreau published *Walden* in 1854, but it was little noticed before his death in 1862.

1845-55

Clipper ships rule the seas. The most successful of these large, fast ships were built at Boston by Donald McKay, whose *Flying Cloud*, launched in 1851, set a record for the voyage from Boston to San Francisco; its elapsed time was eighty-nine days, eight hours. At first clippers brought tea from China; then they took "forty niners" and their supplies to California.

1846 Manchester becomes New Hampshire's first incorporated city. In the decades ahead, **Amoskeag Mills** constructs forty-five acres of buildings along the Merrimack River and employs as many as 17,000 people.

Ether is used as a total anesthetic in surgery by William Morton at Massachusetts General Hospital.

The **sewing machine** is patented by Elias Howe, Jr. After Isaac Singer and others perfected and mass-produced sewing machines, Howe became so wealthy that he personally financed a regiment of Union soldiers in the Civil War.

1848 **Boston imports water** from a pond in its western suburbs. When the valve was opened a fountain of water from Lake Cochituate shot eighty feet into the air above Boston Common's Frog Pond. In 1878 the upper Sudbury River was added to the supply. The Wachusett Reservoir was put into service in 1898 and the Quabbin Reservoir in 1946.

Connecticut Mutual is America's first **life insurance** company.

Samuel Colt comes to Hartford to build a factory to make revolvers, which he patented in 1836. The discovery of gold in California assured the success of this factory, which made 60,000 handguns in 1858.

Vermont gets railroads from Rutland to Burlington, and from White River Junction to Bethel.

1849 Maine ships over five million feet of **lumber** to California. The state's old growth pines were soon depleted.

John White Webster becomes the only Harvard professor ever hanged. He had killed Dr. George Parkman and burned his body at the medical school.

1850 A national **woman's rights convention** takes place at Worcester and proposes allowing women to vote.

The federal government's **Fugitive Slave Law** gives rise to the underground railroad, a network of routes through which escaping slaves were assisted in reaching Canada.

The **chewing gum** industry begins when John B. Davis makes spruce gum in Portland, Maine.

The immediate success of Nathaniel Hawthorne's *The Scarlet Letter* is partially due to its rather daring subject matter—the scarlet letter was an "A," for adultery.

Northern New England's big **log drives** on the Penobscot, Kennebec, and other rivers take place in the second half of this century.

1851 Maine prohibits the manufacture and sale of **alcoholic beverages** with a law that remained in force until 1934. By the mid 1850s all of New England was dry, but alcohol was legal again by 1868 in each state except Maine.

1852 At New Hampshire's **Lake Winnepesaukee**, Harvard defeats Yale in the first intercollegiate rowing contest.

1856 **Electroplating of metal** is invented at Hartford by Asa H. Williams and Simeon S. Rogers.

1857 The magazine *Atlantic Monthly* begins publication under editor James Russell Lowell.

The **coldest morning of the nineteenth century** is January 24, when temperatures reached fifty degrees below zero in Vermont and thirty below in Boston's suburbs.

1859 Educator and philosopher **John Dewey** is born in Burlington, Vermont.

On January 4 deep snow falls throughout New England. Hartford was buried by thirty-six inches, and Goffstown, New Hampshire, received thirty inches in twelve hours.

1860 **Shoe workers** in Lynn, Massachusetts, strike for higher wages and union representation. The strike spread to twenty-five towns and won a raise but not a union.

1861 The **American Civil War** begins. The Sixth Massachusetts, the first full regiment to answer Lincoln's call for troops, rushed to defend Washington. Ambrose Burnside was close behind with a thousand men from Rhode Island.

A wagon road to the summit of **Mount Washington** is completed from a base to the west of the peak. The Cog Railroad was built in 1869 on the mountain's east side.

1862 **Henry David Thoreau** dies of tuberculosis. Emerson's speech at the funeral included this thought:

> He declined to give up his large ambition of knowledge and action for any narrow craft or profession, aiming at a much more comprehensive calling, the art of living well... He chose to be rich by making his wants few, and supplying them himself.

1863 A **Confederate privateer** disguised as a fishing boat brings the Civil War to Portland Harbor. The Confederates stole the lightly guarded Federal ship *Caleb Cushing*. They nearly succeeded at sailing her out of the harbor, but the wind died and left them at the mercy of steam-powered pursuit. Before surrendering, the Confederates scuttled the *Cushing*.

1864 At St. Albans, Vermont, the **northern-most action of the Civil War** takes place when twenty-two Confederate soldiers rob banks and flee to Canada with $20,000.

1865 The **Civil War is over**. Half of Vermont's eligible men served, and a quarter of these were lost.

1866 In Portland, Maine, a Fourth of July celebration starts a **fire** that leaves 10,000 families homeless.

1869 **Gypsy moths** escape from an amateur entomologist in Medford, Massachusetts. In the course of the next century they spread north to Canada, south to Virginia, and west to the Middle West. In any given area their populations fluctuate; where they are numerous, gypsy moth caterpillars devour every leaf from entire forests.

1871 Missouri native Samuel Clemens, known by his pen name **Mark Twain**, moves to Hartford. Twain's books include *Tom Sawyer, A Connecticut Yankee in King Arthur's Court,* and *Huckleberry Finn*; the latter is often considered his masterpiece. Twain collaborated with another Hartford writer, Charles Dudley Warner, on *The Gilded Age*.

One of Twain's neighbors was another famous writer, **Harriet Beecher Stowe**, author of *Uncle Tom's Cabin*, which was published before the Civil War and did much to excite public opinion against slavery.

R. W. Emerson takes a railroad trip to the far west, visiting Yosemite and lecturing in San Francisco.

1873 **Earmuffs** are invented by Chester Greenwood of Farmington, Maine. Greenwood mass-produced them in a factory in that town.

1874 The **Minute Man Statue** by Daniel Chester French is placed at the North Bridge in Concord, Massachusetts, for dedication the following April at the centennial of the bridge fight.

1875 The original **baseball glove** is used by a first baseman for a Boston team.

New Hampshire's White Mountains become a popular summer resort and a railroad is completed to Crawford Notch.

1876 The **telephone is patented** by Alexander Graham Bell of Boston. The first telephone conversation was between Bell and his associate, Thomas Watson.

In April Boston's baseball team wins the first official game of the National League, defeating Philadelphia six to five.

Ivy league colleges meet at Springfield, Massachusetts, to discuss the rules for the new sport of **football**.

The **Appalachian Mountain Club** is organized in Boston to promote hiking and conservation.

1877 Boston's **Trinity Church** is completed in Copley Square. Designed in 1872 by famed architect Henry Hobson Richardson, Trinity Church typifies an architectural style called Romanesque Revival or Richardson Romanesque.

1878 The first Columbia **bicycle** is built in Hartford. By the turn of the century Columbia employed 3800 people and manufactured an automobile called the Columbia Electric Phaeton.

1880 As **deforestation reaches its peak**, the landscape of southern New England is nearly treeless. Farming began a slow decline and the demand for cordwood fell as other fuels became available. Pastures and hay fields were abandoned and began to grow back into forests.

1881 A **telephone** line is installed between Boston and Providence, Rhode Island.

The **Boston Symphony Orchestra** is founded by Major Henry Lee Higginson.

September 6 is known as the "**Yellow Day**" because the light is tinted by smoke from forest fires in Michigan.

The last **mountain lion** in Vermont is killed.

Clara Barton founds the **American Red Cross**. She served as its president until 1904. Barton, born in North Oxford, Massachusetts, had risen to prominence as a nurse in the Civil War.

1884 The United States **Naval War College** is established at Newport, Rhode Island.

1800s

1885 An electrical **transformer** is invented by William Stanley in Great Barrington, Massachusetts.

Robert Frost, his mother, and sister move from San Francisco to Lawrence, Massachusetts. Frost became New England's most popular modem poet.

1888 A three-wheeled electric **automobile** designed by Philip Prate is built in Boston by the Kimball Company.

New England is beset by a blizzard from March 11 to March 14.

1889 America's second **trolley** is built in Bangor, Maine. Richmond, Virginia, had one the year before.

The **Underwood Typewriter** Company begins production in Hartford.

Ice cutters

1890 **Refrigeration** still depends on ice cut from ponds during the winter. This year, Maine's ice exports total 3,000,000 tons.

1890-1914

These are the glory years of the lavish summer homes built in Newport by wealthy railroad and banking families such as the Vanderbilts and the Astors. Bar Harbor, Maine, was another major summer social capital.

1891 **Basketball** is invented by James Naismith in Springfield, Massachusetts.

1892 Charles and Frank Duryea privately test America's first successful **gasoline powered automobile** at Chicopee, Massachusetts. The next year they ran a more powerful design in public at Springfield. By the turn of the century the Stevens-Duryea Company of Chicopee Falls was one of a dozen automobile manufacturers in the United States.

Duryea automobile, 1890s

The **Church of Christ Scientist** is founded in Boston by Mary Baker Eddy.

1894 **Town histories** are published by many New England communities in this era. Henry Nourse, historian of Harvard, Massachusetts, wrote:

> The locomotive has brought many advantages to the community, and also some false ambitions, morbid appetites and artificial tastes; and borne away much simplicity in life and manners without compensation in human happiness.

1895 At the YMCA in Holyoke, Massachusetts, William Moran devises the game of **volleyball**.

1897 The first **Boston Marathon** is won by John McDermott of New York City. His time was two hours, fifty-five minutes, and ten seconds.

Boston's new **subway** is the first in America.

1898 A tremendous storm strikes the New England coast in November. The "**Portland Gale**" wrecked 141 vessels, took 456 lives, and rearranged the coastline.

1899 Half of America's **shoe**s are made in Massachusetts.

In August, Mr. and Mrs. F.O. Stanley of Newton, Massachusetts make the first **automobile ascent of Mount Washington**—in a vehicle powered by steam.

1900s

1900 **Half of Boston's population is Irish** or of Irish descent, and only a tenth is of English ancestry.

1902 The **Mount Washington Hotel** opens at Bretton Woods, New Hampshire, offering lavish accommodations for 550. Amenities included a fabulous view of its namesake mountain, ballrooms, shops, and an indoor swimming pool. At this time large hotels designed to serve affluent summer visitors were thriving throughout the mountains of northern Vermont and New Hampshire.

1903 Baseball's first **World Series** is played in Boston. The Boston Pilgrims defeated the Pittsburgh Pirates.

1905 President Theodore Roosevelt meets with leaders from Russia and Japan in Portsmouth, New Hampshire, to negotiate an end to the Russo-Japanese War.

1906 The **San Francisco Earthquake** and subsequent fire cost Hartford insurance companies $18,000,000.

1910 The Green Mountain Club starts laying out the **Long Trail** through Vermont's mountains.

1911 Religious leader Frank W. Sandford predicts that the world will end this year. Sandford has gathered hundreds of converts from all over the world into a community called Shiloh, near Freeport, Maine. The group was known as "The Kingdom, Incorporated," or "the Holy Ghost and Us Society," or "Sandfordism." Sandford, who was a semiprofessional baseball player before he became a Baptist minister, bought a ship called the *Coronet* and sailed from Portland to Jerusalem, where he took aboard a passenger who later prosecuted him for detaining her against her will. Sandford was convicted and served time in the federal penitentiary in Atlanta but resumed preaching after his release.

1900s

1912   A **workman's compensation** law is passed in Rhode Island to provide medical care and pay to those injured at their jobs.

Textile workers **strike** at Lawrence, Massachusetts.

Leon Leonwood Bean starts making hunting boots with rubber bottoms and leather tops. Beginning with $400 capital, he will build a giant mail order and retail business in Freeport, Maine.

1914   The **Cape Cod Canal** opens to vessels drawing less than fifteen feet. In 1940 the canal was deepened to thirty feet.

1916   The **Massachusetts Institute of Technology**, which was started in Boston in 1861, moves to its new campus in Cambridge.

1917   **John Fitzgerald Kennedy** is born in Brookline, Massachusetts.

1918   A terrible **flu epidemic** strikes Boston and other eastern cities in early September and spreads across the nation, killing nearly 500,000 people.

1919   **Molasses** drowns twenty-one people in Boston after a storage tank bursts, releasing a wave of syrup twenty feet high.

Acadia National Park is established when Congress accepts a gift of land on Mount Desert Island, mostly on and around Cadillac Mountain, creating the first national park east of the Mississippi River. At first it was called Lafayette National Park, but in 1928 the name was changed to Acadia. Additional land, including much of the Isle au Haut, was later added to the park.

1920s

The **textile industry** declines in New England as plants move to southern states. By 1935 Fall River, Massachusetts, had lost half its payroll and three-fourths of its textile industry.

1924 Even rural New Englanders are buying automobiles as the price of the **Ford Model T** hits bottom at $240, and Ford makes its ten millionth car.

1927 Serious **flood**s strike the Winooski River, the Connecticut River, and its Vermont tributaries, resulting in sixty fatalities. Because the ground was already frozen, heavy November rains from a tropical storm caused streams and rivers to overflow their banks.

1929 *Birds of Massachusetts and Other New England States*, a monumental three-volume work, is completed by Edward Howe Forbush and published by the Massachusetts Department of Agriculture. Forbush died on March 7.

1930 **Electricity** has been provided to only half of New England's farms by this date.

The **Woods Hole Oceanographic Institution** is formed on Cape Cod to advance marine sciences. Because of its stimulating intellectual atmosphere and high level of interdisciplinary cooperation, Woods Hole is cited as a model research center.

1933 For her performance in *Morning Glory*, Hartford native **Katherine Hepburn** wins an Academy Award. She will win three more Oscars in the course of her long career.

1934 New England's first **ski tow**, powered by a Model T Ford, begins pulling skiers uphill at Woodstock, Vermont. Recreational skiing mushroomed in the 1940s, to the economic benefit of northern New England.

February 9 is the **coldest morning of the twentieth century** in southern New England. In Boston and Providence the temperature was eighteen degrees below zero. On April 2, the highest wind velocity ever measured anywhere in the world, 231 miles per hour, was recorded at the weather observatory atop Mount Washington.

1900s

1936 **Tanglewood**, an estate owned by a Boston businessman, is given to Serge Koussevitzky as the summer home of the Boston Symphony Orchestra.

1938 On September 21, the **Great New England Hurricane** sweeps through the region, causing massive damage and killing 258 Rhode Islanders and more than 600 in all. At the Blue Hill Observatory in Milton, Massachusetts, winds were measured at 121 miles per hour with gusts to 186 miles per hour. Many, many trees were blown down by this storm. Along the shore, houses were washed as much as a half mile inland by storm waves.

1942 In Boston, the **Cocoanut Grove nightclub fire** kills 492 people in twelve minutes.

1944 The **International Monetary Conference** is held at the Mount Washington Hotel, laying the groundwork for postwar economic development. The International Monetary Fund and the World Bank were planned at the conference.

1947-48 In the **snowiest winter** ever recorded for southern New England, Boston's snowfall totals 89.2 inches, and Providence receives 75.6 inches.

1953 On June 9, a **tornado** slashes through central Massachusetts, injuring 1299 and taking 94 lives in Worcester and neighboring towns.

1954 **Hurricane Carol** visits New England on August 31.

1955 Floods from **Hurricanes Connie and Diane** take eighty-two lives and result in a series of flood control measures, including the construction of a new dam at the mouth of the Charles River in Boston.

1960 Commercial production of **nuclear power** begins at Rowe, Massachusetts.

1960s
In this and the following decades, **agriculture all but disappears** in broad areas of southern New England. Small towns within commuting distance of urban centers were rapidly suburbanized.

1960 Massachusetts Senator **John F. Kennedy** is elected 35th President of the United States. He was assasinated in Dallas, Texas, in 1963

1966 The **Cape Cod National Seashore** is established in response to the growing demand for government protection of fragile natural environments.

1969 **Interstate 95** is completed across Rhode Island, and the Newport Bridge over Narragansett Bay links Newport with Jamestown, Rhode Island.

1970 By establishing the **Environmental Control Law**, Vermont takes the lead among New England states in protecting the public's interest in land use issues.

1979 Construction of additional **nuclear power** plants is prohibited by the Connecticut legislature, reflecting the controversy that has come to surround this source of electricity. Three such plants were already in operation in Connecticut.

1980s
As the **computer industry** reaches its peak of expansion and profitability, the region's economy soars, but by the end of the decade the boom was over.

1992 Despite the objections of Connecticut Governor Lowell Weicker, the **Mashantucket Pequot tribe opens Foxwoods**, a casino, in the town of Ledyard.

1998 The **Great Ice Storm** damages forests and the electricity grid, resulting in lengthy power outages in parts of New England and eastern Canada.

2000s

2000 Vermont is the first state to legally recognize **civil unions** between partners of the same sex.

2001 In the terrorist attacks of **September 11**, two flights that departed from Boston's Logan Airport for Los Angeles are hijacked by terrorists. One was deliberately crashed into each of the twin towers of the World Trade Center, causing the collapse of the buildings and enormous loss of life.

2003 The Massachusetts Supreme Judicial Court decides that the Commonwealth could not deny marriage rights to gay couples under the state constitution. The following year the court ruled that allegedly separate but equal civil unions, as implemented in Vermont, were not sufficient; that only full **gay marriage** rights met constitutional requirments. The decision took effect in May, 2004.

A **nightclub fire** in West Warwick, Rhode Island takes 100 lives.

2004 The **Boston Red Sox win their first baseball World Series** in eighty-six years, ending what had been termed "the curse of the Bambino"; the supposed result of the team's sale of Babe Ruth to the New York Yankees.

2005 The Boston Central Artery/Tunnel Project is completed. The so-called "**Big Dig**" put an elevated highway underground and made other improvements to the city's appearance and accessibility.

2011   As waters warm, predators disappear, and conservation pays off, **Maine's lobster harvest** exceeds 100 million pounds.

2012   Adam Lanza shoots and kills 26 people at **Sandy Hook Elementary School** in Newtown, Connecticut, a most heartbreaking challenge to America's numbness about gun violence.

2013   The **Boston Marathon terrorist attack**. Two bombs exploded near the finish line in Boston. Three people were killed and hundreds injured by bombers Dzhokhar and Tamerlan Tsarnaev.

American Natives and English Colonists

Human beings wandered into New England after the retreat, some fifteen thousand years ago, of a mile-deep sheet of glacial ice. About two thousand years ago, the Algonquin people entered this region from the Midwest, bringing with them knowledge of pottery, the bow and arrow, and agriculture. The Algonquins became the dominant cultural influence, although it is unknown whether this took place through gradual assimilation or by warfare. When Europeans arrived, all American natives from the Maritime Provinces to North Carolina spoke languages of the Eastern Algonquian family.

Native farmers grew maize, beans, tobacco, and squash, including pumpkins and zucchini. They made extensive use of fish, shellfish, and marine mammals and gathered berries, nuts, seeds, and roots. They hunted deer, bear, beaver, raccoon, rabbit, and muskrat. Their homes were wigwams, framed with bent saplings and covered with mats or bark.

At the time of first contact with Europeans some 500 years ago, the land that was to become Massachusetts was home to the Nipmuck, Pawtucket, Massachusetts, and Wampanoag. Forest management by fire was practiced—annual burning of the underbrush eased foot travel and encouraged food producing plants such as strawberries, raspberries, and blackberries without destroying the oaks, hickories, and chestnuts that also generated valuable food for human beings and their prey animals.

In 1614, John Smith explored New England. A second vessel on the expedition was commanded by Thomas Hunt, who kidnapped twenty native men at Plymouth and seven more at Cape Cod, and sold them as slaves in Spain. One of those enslaved was a man named Squanto, who traveled from Spain to England and eventually to Newfoundland where, in 1618, he boarded a ship on its way to trade in Massachusetts.

During Squanto's absence, disaster had struck. An epidemic had swept away the majority of the native Americans living along the coast. Between Saco Bay in Maine and Narragansett Bay in Rhode Island, the population of native coastal peoples declined from 100,000 in 1617 to 5,000 by 1619. The disease is suspected to have been a European childhood illness such as chicken pox or measles. English settlers thought that Divine Providence had removed the biggest obstacle to New England's settlement and left cleared fields for their convenience.

In 1621 the Pilgrims were pleasantly surprised to meet Squanto, who was able to translate during their successful negotiations with the Wampanoag sachem, Massasoit.

The fact that the Pilgrims were able to live peacefully with their native neighbors emboldened restless Puritans back in England. They obtained a charter for their Massachusetts Bay Colony in 1629, which granted them all of the land from three miles south of the Charles River to three miles north of the Merrimack River and west to the "South Sea," as the Pacific Ocean was then named. Six ships delivered 406 people to Salem. Some of these moved on to establish Charlestown at the mouth of the Charles River.

The hilly land between the lower Charles and the harbor, now the site of Boston, was called Shawmut Peninsula. The first white person to live there was William Blackstone, who moved there from Plymouth Colony in about 1624. Puritan immigrants led by John Winthrop settled on the opposite side of the river in 1629 but joined Blackstone on his peninsula in 1630. William Wood observed, "It being a Necke and bare of wood, they are not troubled with three great annoyances of Woolves, Rattlesnakes, and Musketoes." In 1631 Blackstone sold his holdings to the Puritans and moved to what would become Rhode Island.

Because the Shawmut Peninsula was dominated by a hill with three summits, the settlement was at first called Trimountain. In September of 1630 it was renamed Boston after a town in England, home of some of the colonists. Tremont Street reflects the original name. In 1635, a beacon was erected on the highest of the hills to warn of danger. The beacon was a barrel of pitch set atop a pole. The pitch was to have been ignited in the event of enemy attack. The light was never used, but the name of Beacon Hill has endured.

One of the objectives in the king's charter of the Massachusetts Bay Company was the conversion of the Indians to Christianity. Roxbury's minister, John Eliot, took up this task. In October of 1646 Eliot rode to Nonantum, a stockaded Indian village on the south side of the Charles not far from Watertown. The people of Nonantum were a subtribe of the Massachusetts led by a sachem named Waban.

Waban was surrounded by potential enemies: the Nipmucks to the west, the Wampanoags and Narragansetts to the south, and the English to the north and east. Waban apparently felt it wise to ally himself with the English, and in John Eliot he found a sympathetic and effective liaison. He requested that his people be "granted" the land on which they lived. Eliot proposed this to the General Court, and it was done. But it was soon evident that Nonantum was too near the English towns. Some of the whites were willing to exploit their Indian neighbors. At Eliot's suggestion the General Court in 1648 prohibited the selling of spirits to the Indians. A search for a suitable site for an Indian town was begun.

Following months of scouting for a favorable location, Natick was agreed upon. The General Court granted the Indians 2,000 acres to the north of the Charles, but the Indians settled on both sides of the river and built a bridge. Dedham sued to evict the Indians from the south bank, but the General Court let the Indians stay and gave Dedham 8,000 acres in Deerfield as compensation. Natick still straddles the Charles.

The Indians' bridge spanned an eighty-foot river. Its central arch was nine feet high. This footbridge outlasted floods and stood unbroken for many years, to the pride of Indian residents. William Tilden wrote: "[Medfield's] earliest bridge over Charles River, a little way above the present poorfarm bridge, was carried away by a freshet; Eliot's Indians had built a bridge at Natick about the same time; and they plumed themselves greatly that their bridge stood, while that at Medfield was washed away."

At first the Indians lived in wigwams. A sawmill was established on Waban Brook, and English-style carpentry was begun, but many Indians found wigwams warmer and more comfortable.

John Eliot established the first Natick government along a Biblical plan, using the system given to Moses by Jethro. One man was chosen out of every ten to judge small matters. The hierarchy ascended to leaders of fifty and to a single patriarch to settle major disputes. An elderly man named Totherswamp was the highest ruler. Waban was one of the rulers of fifty. A warrant he issued has been preserved: "You big constable, quick you catch him, Jeremiah Offscoe; strong you hold him; safe you bring him afore me. Thomas Waban, Justice Peace."

Whether or not we are sympathetic with John Eliot's efforts to imbue the natives with English culture, the fact that he cared about their welfare makes him stand out, and his gentleness, his incredible energy and diligence mark him as heroic. He was born in August, 1604, at Widford, Hertfordshire, England. He received a degree from Jesus

College, Cambridge, in 1622. Puritan friends invited him to move to Massachusetts with them as their minister. Eliot sailed in the ship *Lyon* and reached Boston in November, 1631, in the company of Governor Winthrop's wife and children. Eliot married Ann Mumford in October of 1632. When his friends from Essex arrived and settled in Roxbury, Eliot joined them. He ministered to their church for nearly sixty years.

In 1641 Eliot hired an Indian named Cockenoe to translate for him and to teach him the Algonquian tongue. On October 28, 1646, he preached at Nonantum and began his association with Waban's people. News of Eliot's work was published in England, where there was more sympathy with Native Americans than there was among English in the New World. In 1649 Parliament created the Society for the Propagation of the Gospel in New England. Every house in England was canvassed, making Eliot famous as "Apostle to the Indians." In the first year, £12,000 was collected and invested. The income supported Eliot's work.

At the same time that he was establishing Natick, Eliot decided that the Indians must have a Bible in their own language. The fact that this language had never been written did not discourage him. Eliot devised a phonetic system for writing and reading Algonquian and began the enormous task of translation. His work is a valuable record for linguists. The Natick Dictionary, published in 1903 by the U.S. Government Printing Office, lists many translations including *umshuu*, a canoe; *paugaremissaund*, an oak canoe; *wompmissaund*, a chestnut canoe; and *wawaund*, a pine canoe.

Eliot's New Testament translation was published in 1661 and the Old Testament in 1663. It was the first Bible published in North America. Eliot preached at Natick every other week until he was too feeble from old age to ride out from Roxbury.

The success of Natick encouraged Eliot and his associates to create other towns. By 1674 they had established fourteen towns modeled after Natick, with a combined population of about 1100. The Indian town of Hassanamasitt became Grafton. Okommakamesit is now Marlborough, Wamesitt was at Lowell, Nashobah at Littleton. Magunkaquog became Ashland. Machage, Chabanakong-kowun, Maanexit, and Quantisset were to the west, in Nipmuck territory. Wabquissit was seventy-two miles from Boston, but Eliot travelled to each, and made a tour of all fourteen in 1674. This was a farewell visit, because King Philip's War brought it all down.

In 1675 relations between the English and the Indians collapsed, and the Wampanoag sachem Metacomet, or Philip, led an attempt to extinguish the Massachusetts Bay Colony. Hostilities commenced in July with Indian attacks on Swansea and Mendon. Though whites outnumbered the Indians, in the fall of 1675 the English were forced to face the possibility of their annihilation, as the towns of Brookfield, Dartmouth, Deerfield, Groton, Lancaster, Mendon, Middleborough, Northfield, Simsbury, Warwick, Wickford, Worcester, and Wrentham were destroyed. The Indians held the advantage during the winter and spring, but their efforts weakened as they depleted the supplies of the villages they had captured and their own towns and crops were burned by the whites.

In October of 1675 the Christian Indians were removed to Deer Island in Boston Harbor "For their and our security." Eliot wrote that his people were "Harried away to an island at half an hour's warning, poor souls in terror they left their goods, books, Bibles, only some few carried their Bibles; the rest were spoiled and lost. The profane Indians prove a sharp rod to the English, and the English prove a very sharp rod to the praying Indians."

Most of Metacomet's warriors dispersed or surrendered during the summer of 1676, and Metacomet was killed in August. Massachusetts and Plymouth lost 600 people and fifty towns. The Indian losses were about 3000, approximately one-third of their population. Most Indian captives were executed or sold into slavery in the West Indies.

After the war, the surviving Indians returned and rebuilt Natick. The Indian character of the town faded slowly; the last Indian officeholder left his position in 1745, and by 1764 the fifty-six white families outnumbered the Indians. By 1787 little land remained in Indian hands.

New England and the War for Independence

Militia from Boston and nearby towns fought the first two battles of the American War for Independence: Lexington and Concord, and Bunker Hill. The chain of events leading to these engagements stemmed from New England's stubborn demands for liberty. The final conflict began in 1765 when, in an attempt to raise money to pay debts from the French and Indian War, the British Parliament passed a Stamp Act requiring Americans to purchase stamps for legal and business papers, pamphlets, and newspapers. This failed but was followed in 1767 by the Townshend Acts, which taxed glass, paper, paints, and tea. In 1768 British troops were sent to Boston, which had become a hotbed of resistance to the authority of the mother country.

The presence of troops led to the Boston Massacre in 1770. Under attack by a stone-throwing mob, British soldiers opened fire, killing five people. Although they were tried in Boston, the soldiers, defended in court by John Adams, were found to have acted in self-defense. Nevertheless, Patriots generated propaganda from the incident. A Boston newspaper printed Paul Revere's engraving of the shooting of "unarmed" citizens. The British government cancelled all of the Townshend Act taxes except for a small levy on tea.

Continued resistance to "taxation without representation" brought on the Boston Tea Party in 1773. The night before three ships of British-owned tea were to be unloaded, Sam Adams held a public meeting at the Old South Meeting House. On Adams's cue, "This meeting can do nothing more to save the country," the Sons of Liberty went to the wharf and dumped 342 chests of tea into the harbor. Paul Revere was one of the participants.

In response to Boston's refusal to pay for this tea, Parliament passed the "Intolerable Acts" in 1774, closing the port of Boston, suspending the Massachusetts legislature, and placing the colony under the rule of General Gage, who arrived in Boston with additional troops. The general's authority was effective only within the city; the rest of the colony formed its own government. Companies of Patriot militia began training in towns throughout New England. The colonies prepared for united action by holding a Continental Congress; John Adams represented Massachusetts.

In 1775, British troops were dispatched from Boston to seize munitions stored in Concord. Patriot leaders had anticipated this move, and companies of local militia called Minute Men had trained to meet such an emergency. When the British troop movement began on the night of April 18, a young Patriot from Boston, William Dawes, slipped by the British sentries and rode through Roxbury, Brookline, Cambridge, and Menotomy (Arlington) on his way to Lexington, spreading the alarm as he went.

Two lanterns were hung in the steeple of Christ Church (now called Old North) to signal Patriots in Charlestown that the redcoats were moving by boat up the river rather than marching via Boston Neck. Meanwhile, Paul Revere was rowed across the mouth of the Charles River and lent a horse so that he could ride to Lexington. The bell in the Lexington meetinghouse called out the Minute Men. Revere was stopped by a British patrol, but Dr. Samuel Prescott carried the warning to Concord.

British troops disembarked at East Cambridge in the early hours of April 19 and, after a long delay, began their march through what are now Somerville and Arlington. The column was confronted at dawn on Lexington Green by the town's Minute Men, under Captain Parker, who ordered his seventy-seven men to "Stand your ground! Don't fire unless fired upon! But if they mean to have a war, let it begin here!"

The British commander, Major Pitcairn, shouted to the Minute Men, "Lay down your arms, you damned rebels, and disperse!" With his men outnumbered ten to one, Captain Parker was willing to withdraw, but there was a gunshot—no one knows who fired it—followed by a British volley that killed eight Americans.

The British continued to Concord and searched for arms, most of which had been removed from the town or thoroughly hidden. A detachment was sent to the west of the village to guard the North Bridge over the Concord River. When Minute Men on the high ground across the river saw smoke from the village center, they believed that the British were setting fire to the town and they decided to force their way across the bridge. British guards fired from the bridge, and the militia returned fire. There were casualties on both sides, and the surviving British retreated to the center of town.

Colonial militia streamed toward Concord from all directions. By the time the scarlet-clad column began its withdrawal toward Boston, it was surrounded by hostile forces. For the most part the Americans were kept out of musket range of the column by British flankers, but where militia gained positions near the road they took a heavy toll. By the time the British reached Charlestown 73 had died and 174 were wounded. The Americans suffered 49 dead and 40 wounded. The British retreated into Boston, and the Americans laid siege to the city.

The Battle of Bunker Hill took place on June 17 after American forces occupied high ground that threatened Boston, forcing the British to cross the Charles River to dislodge them. The redcoats were finally successful in capturing the hill, but they took fearful casualties in doing so, and the Americans' will to fight was demonstrated beyond doubt. To retaliate for sniper fire from the town, the British burned Charlestown.

Shortly after the Battle of Bunker Hill, George Washington arrived from Virginia with riflemen from several colonies. These plus the New Englanders on hand formed the core of what became the Continental Army. Washington established his headquarters in Cambridge. During the following winter, fifty cannon were dragged over the snow from Fort Ticonderoga. In March, Washington placed these cannon on Dorchester Heights, from which they commanded Boston. The British were allowed to depart in safety, with the proviso that they not set fire to the town. Most of Boston's Loyalists left with the troops.

Industry and Idealism

New Englanders were at the forefront of upheavals in the early decades of the 1800s, as businessmen launched America's industrial revolution and writers helped Americans come to terms with the new age.

In Rhode Island, the industrial revolution began with Samuel Slater's activities on the Blackstone River (see page 40). In Massachusetts, it started on the Charles River in Waltham. Water power had been harnessed there for making paper in 1788, but it was textiles that made Waltham famous as a pioneer industrial city, at the initiative of Francis Cabot Lowell and his associates. After studying manufacturing methods in England, Lowell decided to attempt large-scale production of cotton cloth in the United States. He and his partners formed the Boston Manufacturing Company and bought the water privilege at Waltham. They built a five-story building at the fall, which survives as the section of the mill nearest the dam. Lowell hired a skilled and inventive mechanic named Paul Moody to set up the machinery, which included America's first practical power loom.

Production began in 1816. Lowell died the next year, but his Boston Manufacturing Company prospered. The success of the mill at Waltham led the company to seek greater water power to expand its operations, resulting in the establishment of the city of Lowell beside the Merrimack River. At first most of the company's mill workers were young women recruited from farms, but in a few decades immigrants from Europe and Canada came to predominate in the work force. By the time of the Civil War, Lowell was the largest industrial complex in America.

As industrialization proceeded, Boston-area writers and ministers, who became known as Transcendentalists, debated the relationship of nature, human beings, and progress, and tried in a series of utopian experimental communities to live out their high ideals. One such community was Brook Farm. In 1840, George and Sophia Ripley spent a summer on a dairy farm along the Charles River in West Roxbury. Ripley was a Unitarian minister who had concluded that if human beings took action to improve this world, the hereafter would take care of itself. In pursuit of their ideals, Ripley and likeminded associates bought the farm. In a letter to Ralph Waldo Emerson, Ripley explained that the purpose of Brook Farm was:

> . . . to insure a more natural union between intellectual and manual labor than now exists; to combine the thinker and the the worker, as far as possible, in the same individual; to guarantee the highest mental freedom, by providing all with labor adapted to their tastes and talents, and securing to them the fruits of their industry; to do away with the necessity of menial services by opening the benefits of education and the profits of labor to all; and thus to prepare a society of liberal, intelligent, and cultivated persons, whose relationships with each other would permit a more wholesome and simple life than can be led amidst the pressure of our competitive institutions.

In April of 1841 the Ripleys and a dozen others, including Nathaniel Hawthorne, moved to Brook Farm. Transcendentalists who did not live at Brook Farm were very much aware of the experiment that was made there.

Another Transcendentalist, a Unitarian minister named Adin Ballou, initiated the formation of the Hopedale Community. In January of 1841, thirty-two individuals signed its constitution. It was a "joint stock and united industrial association." Ballou and his associates were impatient with the progress of the established church in reform. Ballou wrote:

> Even the more advanced classes in church and state, seeking the progress, the harmony, and happiness of mankind, propose little if anything more than the gradual improvement of society on the old basis of egoism, caste distinctions, competitive rivalry, shrewd and cunning practices, jealousy, and hatred of race and nation.

Ballou's "practical Christian Socialism" had 200 practitioners. The Hopedale Community outlived Brook Farm and was prosperous in 1854 but bankrupt two years later. The community's assets were purchased by Ebenezer and George Draper, who had been involved in its finances. The Draper Company did well producing machinery for milling cotton, and Ballou's group continued as a religious society until 1867.

In June of 1843, Amos Bronson Alcott and his followers and family moved to a farm they called Fruitlands, in the town of Harvard, Massachusetts, where they attempted to create a completely ethical community. Cotton clothing was rejected because cotton was raised by slaves. They did not use leather, because cattle had a right to keep their skins, nor wool, which they thought should be left upon the sheep. Eating meat was out, and although grains and other garden crops were permitted, they were suspect if the soil that grew them had been fertilized with manure or cultivated with the labor of animals. Alcoholic beverages, coffee, tea, and even milk were all scorned; their only drink was water. The Fruitlanders tried to wear only linen, the cloth made from flax, a crop widely grown in Massachusetts. Seeking a food source cultivated by human labor, Alcott and his friends settled on fruit, thus, Fruitlands, though their farm had only a small orchard.

Preparations for the winter were entirely inadequate. The community diminished during the fall and had scattered by January. Unlike the other Transcendentalist experiments, the duration of the Fruitlands venture was measured in months rather than years, but the memory of it is alive because its beautiful site and the original farmhouse are preserved. One of Bronson Alcott's daughters, a willful little girl at the time of her stay at Fruitlands, was Louisa May Alcott, future author of *Little Women*.

Although none of these utopian experiments succeeded as enduring economic enterprises, their participants made themselves heard as defenders of the freedom and dignity of individual human beings. These communities were part of a reform movement that helped America's agrarian society adapt to the industrial revolution.

The Boston Transcendentalists included Ralph Waldo Emerson, born in Boston in 1803, and Nathaniel Hawthorne, born the following year in Salem. Hawthorne became famous as the author of *The Scarlet Letter* and *The House of the Seven Gables*. After an interlude at Brook Farm, Hawthorne married Sophia Peabody, a member of an accomplished Boston family. The first three years of their marriage were spent at the Old Manse in Concord, where Emerson had lived a few years before. The Old Manse is adjacent to Minute Man National Historical Park and is open to visitors.

Emerson waited on tables and taught in secondary schools during the summers to help pay for his studies at Harvard. In 1836 he

The Old Manse, adjacent to Minute Man National Park and the Old North Bridge replica.

published *Nature*, written at the Old Manse, from which the follow excerpt is drawn:

> The greatest delight which the fields and woods minister is the suggestion of an occult relation between man and the vegetable. I am not alone and unacknowledged. They nod to me, and I to them.
>
> The waving of the boughs in the storm is new to me and old. It takes me by surprise, and yet it is not unknown. Its effect is like that of a higher thought or a better emotion coming over me.
>
> Through all its kingdom, to the suburbs and outskirts of things, nature is faithful to the cause whence it had its origin. It always speaks of Spirit. It suggests the absolute. It is a perpetual effect. It is a great shadow pointing always to the sun behind us.

Emerson was a mentor of Henry David Thoreau, now the best known and most widely read of the Transcendentalist writers. Thoreau's solitary stay at Walden Pond began during the Brook Farm years and was in conscious contrast with the farm's sociality. Thoreau was born in Concord in 1817. He lived at Walden Pond from July 4, 1845, until September 6, 1847. He published *Walden* in 1854, but it was little noticed before his death in 1862. Emerson's funeral eulogy included this thought:

> He declined to give up his large ambition of knowledge and action for any narrow craft or profession, aiming at a much more comprehensive calling, the art of living well. . . . He chose to be rich by making his wants few, and supplying them himself.

Thoreau felt that Americans were too much concerned with material undertakings, as expressed in this passage from *Walden*.

> The nation itself, with all its so-called internal improvements, which, by the way, are all external and superficial, is an unwieldy and overgrown establishment, cluttered with furniture, ruined by luxury and heedless expense, by want of calculation and a worthy aim, as are the million households in the land; and the only cure for it, as for them, is in a rigid economy, a seem simplicity of life and an elevation of purpose. It lives too fast. Men think that it is essential that the Nation have commerce, and exports, and talk through a telegraph, and ride thirty miles an hour. . . . If we do not get out sleepers, and forge rails, and devote days and nights to the work, but go to tinkering upon our lives to improve them, who will build railroads? And if railroads are not built, how shall we get to Heaven in season? But if we stay at home and mind our business, who will want railroads? We do not ride on the railroad; it rides upon us.
>
> Why should we live with such hurry and waste of life?

New England

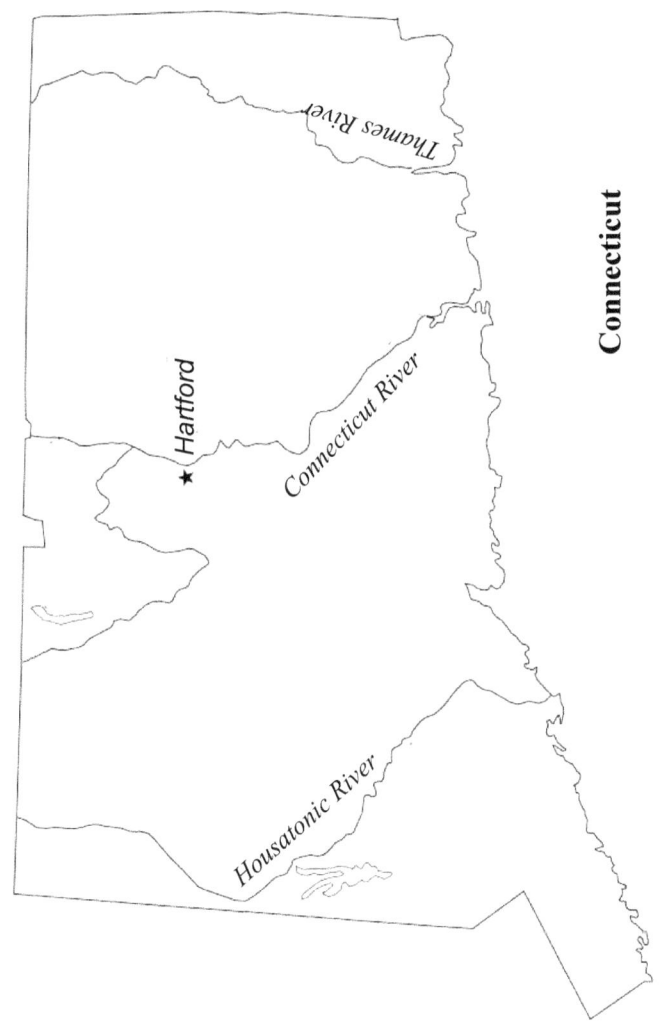

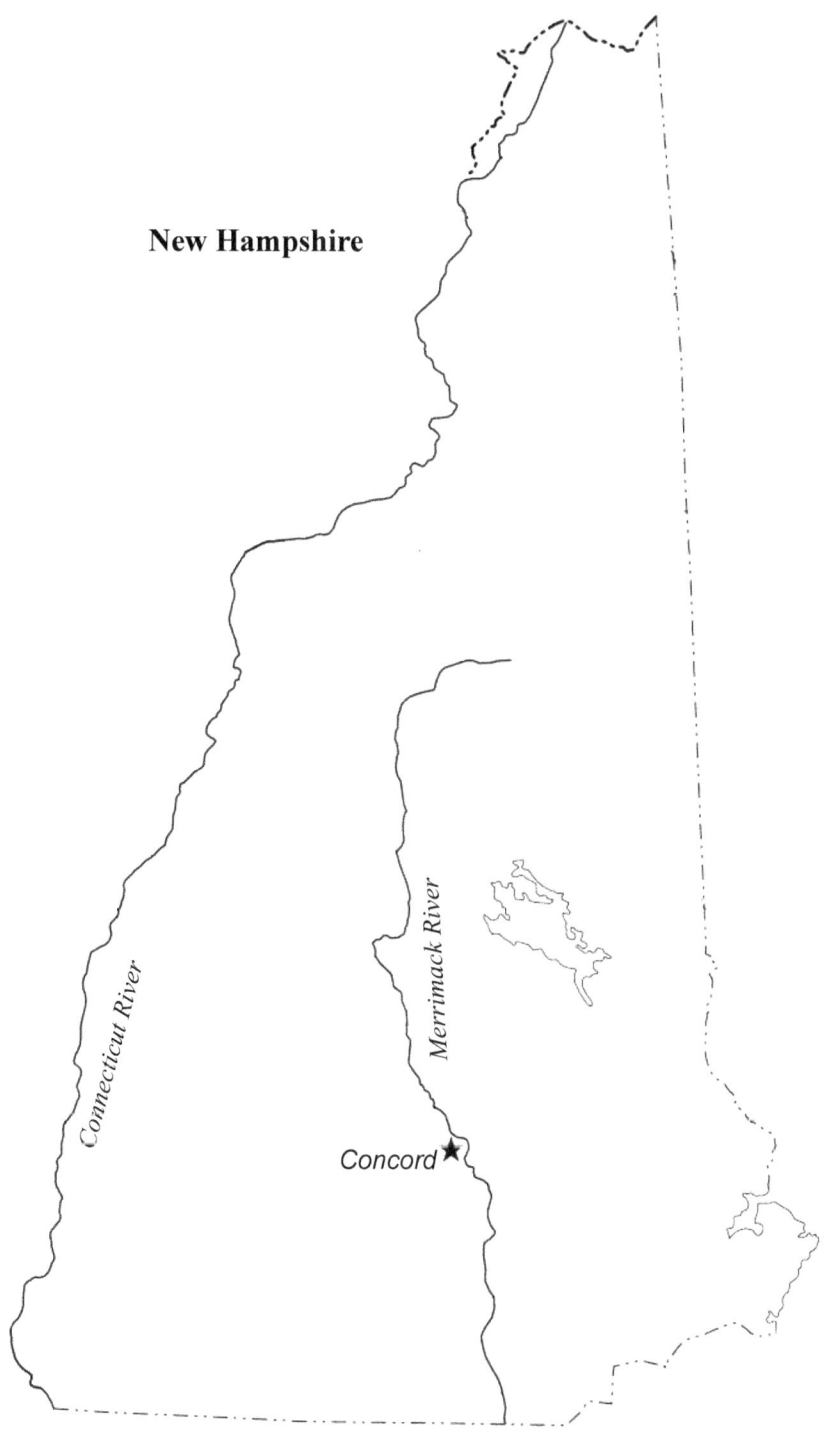

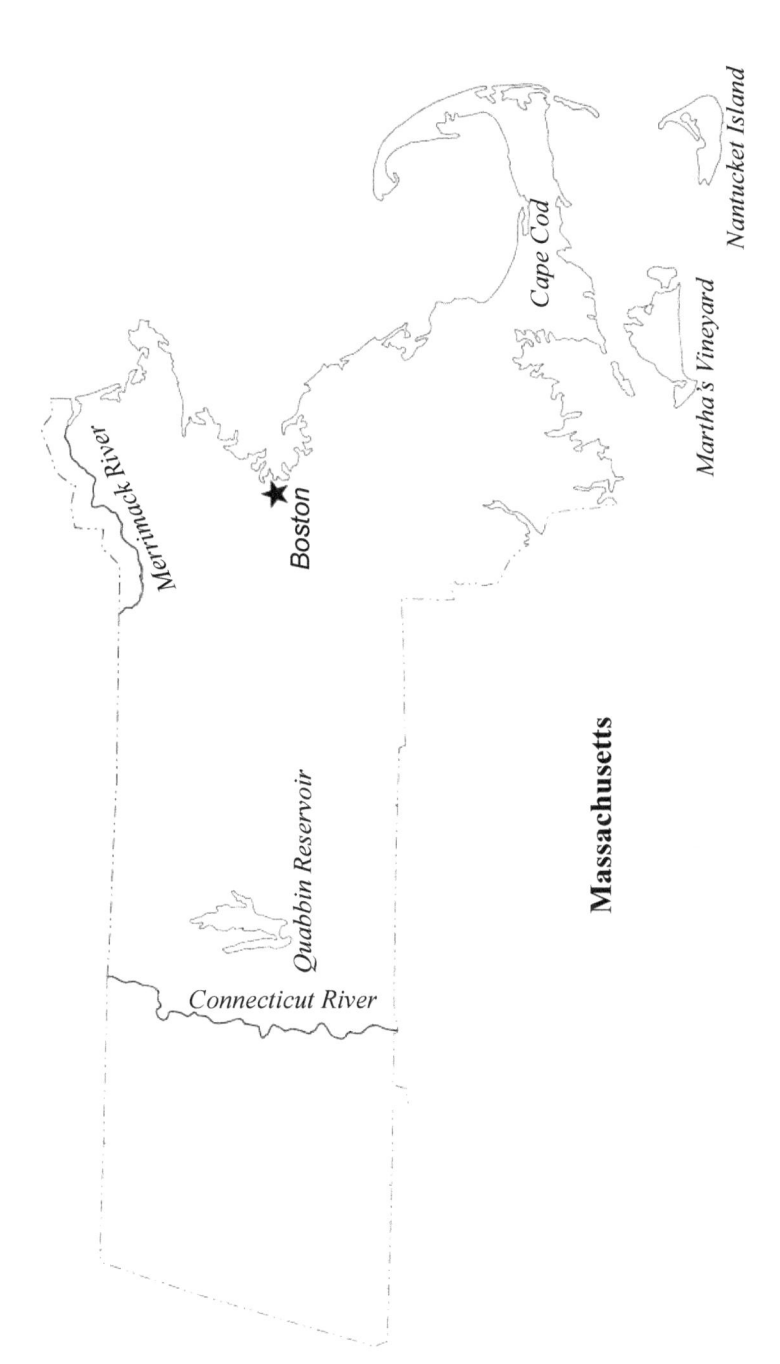

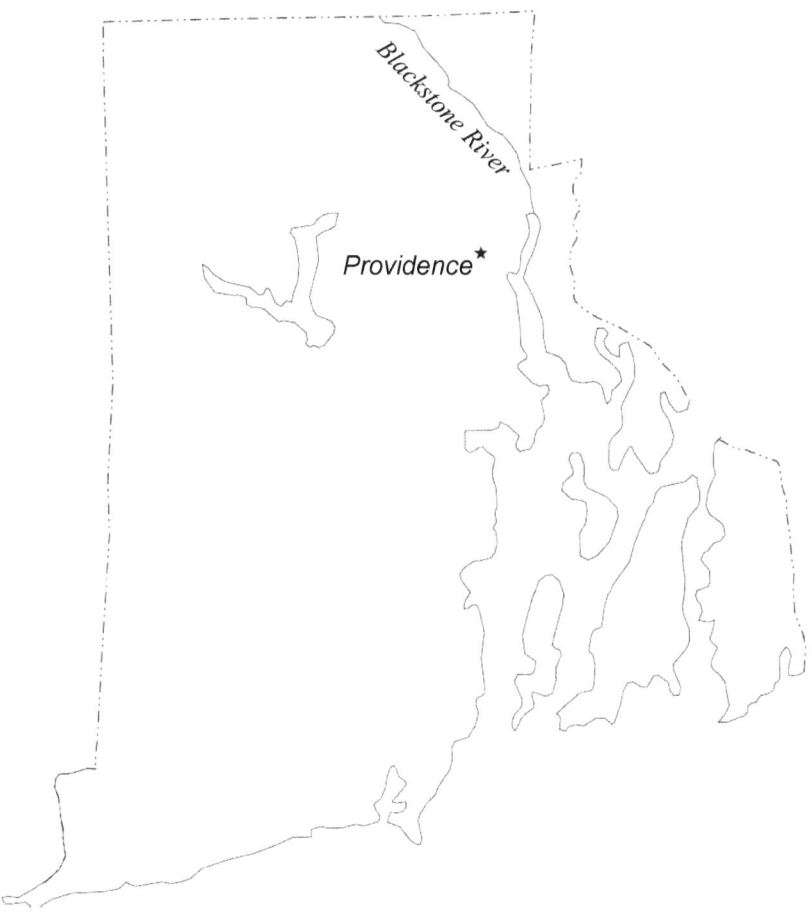

Rhode Island

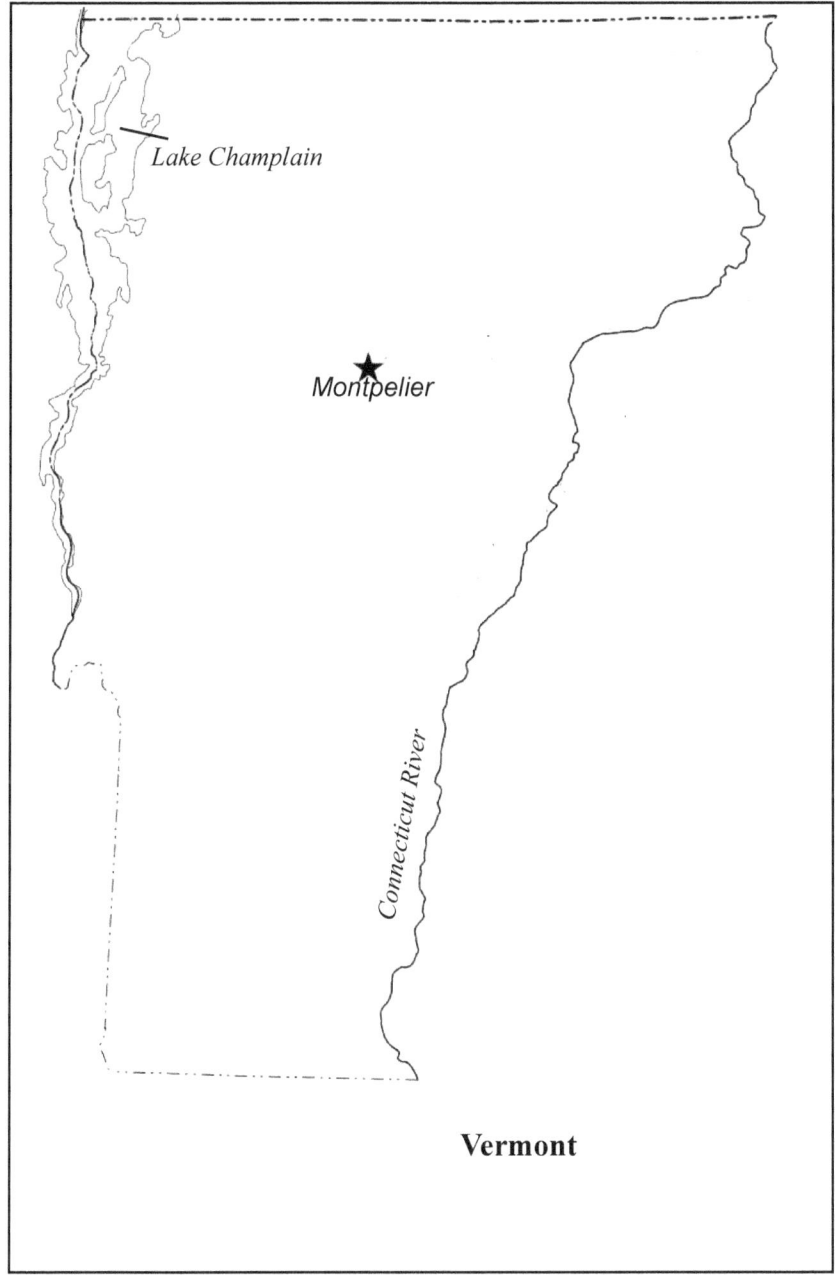

Bibliography

Albion, Robert G, William A. Baker, and Benjamin W. Labaree. *New England and the Sea*. Mystic Seaport: Marine Historical Association, 1972.

Arnold, Samuel Greene. *History of the State of Rhode Island and Providence Plantations*, Volume I. New York: D. Appleton and Company, 1859.

Ballou, Adin. *History of the Hopedale Community*. Lowell: Thompson & Hill, 1897.

Carruth, Gorton. *What Happened When*. New York: Harper & Row, 1989.

Clark, George L. *A History of Connecticut*. New York: G.P. Putnam's Sons, 1914.

Cronon, William. *Changes in the Land*. New York: Hill and Want, 1983.

Drewry, Henry N., Thomas H. O'Connor, Frank Freidel. *America Is*. Columbus, Ohio: Charles E. Merrill Publishing Co., 1982.

Earle, Alice Morse. *Customs and Fashions in Old New England*. New York: Charles Scribner's Sons, 1904.

Fennelly, Catherine. *Life in an Old New England Country Village*. New York: Thomas Y. Crowell Company, 1969.

Finkelstein, Norman H. *The Other 1492*. New York: Charles Scribner's Sons, 1989.

Fiske, John. *The Beginnings of New England*. Houghton, Mifflin and Company, 1897.

Hale, Judson D. "To Patrons," *Old Farmer's Almanac*. Dublin, New Hampshire, 1992.

Hard, Walter. *The Connecticut*. New York: Rinehart & Company, 1947.

Harlow, Alvin F. *Steelways of New England*. New York: Creative Age Press, 1946.

Hemenway, Abby Maria. *Abby Hemenway's Vermont*. Brattleboro, Vermont: The Stephen Greene Press, 1972.

Howe, Henry F. *Massachusetts: There She Is-Behold Her*. New York: Harper and Brothers, 1960.

Howe, Henry F. *Salt Rivers of the Massachusetts Shore*. New York: Rinehart & Company, 1951.

Irland, Lloyd C. *Wildlands and Woodlots*. Hanover: University Press of New England, 1982.

Laska, Vera O. *Remember the Ladies*. Boston: Commonwealth of Massachusetts, 1976.

Laughlin, Clara E. *So You're Seeing New England*. Little, Brown and Company, 1940.

Ludlum, David. *New England Weather Book*. Boston: Houghton Mifflin Company, 1976.

Montgomery, D.H. *The Leading Facts of American History*. Ginn and Company, 1895.

Morison, Samuel Eliot. *Oxford History of the American People.* New York: Oxford University Press, 1965.

Randel, William Peirce. *The Evolution of American Taste*. New York: Crown, 1978.

Rich, Louise Dickinson. *State 0' Maine*. New York: Harper & Row, 1964.

Robinson, William F. *Coastal New England*. Boston: New York Graphic Society, 1983.

Robinson, William F. *Mountain New England*. Boston: Little, Brown, and Company, 1988.

Simmons, William S. *Spirit of the New England Tribes*. Hanover: University Press of New England, 1986.

Simonds, Christopher. *Samuel Slater's Mill and the Industrial Revolution*. Englewood Cliffs, New Jersey: Silver Burdett Press, 1990.

Thomson, Betty Flanders. *The Changing Face of New England*. Boston: Houghton Mifflin Company, 1977.

Vaughan, Alden T., and Edward W. Clark. *Puritans among the Indians* Cambridge: Belknap Press of Harvard University, 1981.

Wagenknect, Edward. *A Pictorial History of New England*. New York: Crown Publishers, 1976.

Wikipedia, The Cloud, 2016

World Book Encyclopedia Chicago:World Book, 1990.

Index

A

Abenaki 2, 20, 22, 24
Acadia 29
Acadia National Park 66
Adams, Abigail 27, 30, 36, 37, 43, 47
Adams, John 30, 31, 32, 38, 43, 47, 77
Adams, John Quincy 30
Adams, Sam 31, 77
Agriculture 2, 44, 69, 72
Alcoholic beverages 18, 40, 50, 55, 58, 74
Alcott, Bronson 52, 55, 82
Alcott, Louisa May 56, 82
Algonquins 2, 72
Allen, Ethan 35
American War for Independence 77
Amherst, Massachusetts 50
Andover, Massachusetts 38
Andros, Sir Edmund 20
Anti-Catholicism 52
Antislavery movement 51
Appalachian Mountain Club 61
April Fool's Day 26
Aquidneck Island 11
Architecture; Federal 43; Georgian 25; Greek Revival 50; Romanesque Revival 61
Arnold, Benedict 35
Aroostook War 54
Atlantic Monthly 58
Augusta, Maine 8, 51
Automobiles 61, 62, 63, 66

B

Ballou, Adin 54, 81
Bangor, Maine 62
Baptists 27
Bar Harbor, Maine 63
Barton, Clara 61
Baseball 60
Battle of Bennington 36
Battle of Lexington and Concord 32
Battle of Saratoga 37
Bay Colony 10, 15
Bay Path 11
Beacon Hill 8, 73
Bean, Leon Leonwood 66
Bell, Alexander Graham 60
Bennington, Vermont 29, 42
Beverly, Massachusetts 8
Bicycles 61
Blackstone River 49, 80
Blackstone, William 8, 9, 73
Block, Adriaen 6
Boston 5, 9, 17, 18, 23, 27, 30, 31, 47, 50, 67, 73; water supply 57
Boston Harbor 26
Boston Manufacturing Company 80
Boston Marathon 64, 71
Boston Massacre 31, 77
Boston Symphony Orchestra 61, 68
Boston Tea Party 31, 77
Boylston, Zabdiel 26
Bradstreet, Anne 6, 16
Brattleboro, Vermont 25
Brook Farm 54, 80, 83
Brown, Moses 40
Brown University 29
Bulfinch, Charles 42, 43
Bunker Hill, Battle of 35, 79
Bunker Hill Monument 50
Burrows, Lieutenant William 46

C

Cabot, John 4
Cadillac Mountain 66
Cajuns 29
Cambridge, Massachusetts 10, 11, 45, 78
Canals 44, 48, 49; Farmington 50;
Canoes 2
Canonicus 11
Cape Ann 5, 6
Cape Cod 1, 4, 6, 20, 72

Cape Cod Canal 66
Cape Cod National Seashore 69
Casco Bay 5
Champlain Canal 48
Champlain, Samuel de 5, 6
Channing, William Ellery 48, 52
Charles River 1, 6, 8, 35, 46, 73, 74, 78, 80
Charlestown, Massachusetts 9, 26, 35, 73, 79
Charlestown Navy Yard 51
Chewing gum 58
Chocolate 30
Christ Church 78
Christian Science 63
Christmas 18, 26
Civil War 26, 44, 57, 59
Clemens, Samuel 60
Clipper ships 56
Cockenoe 75
Cocoanut Grove nightclub fire 68
Coffee 37, 48, 55
Cog Railroad 59
Colt, Samuel 57
Committees of Correspondence 31
Computer industry 69
Concord Coach 50
Concord, Massachusetts 32, 44, 47, 56, 60, 78
Concord, New Hampshire 50
Concord River 78
Connecticut Colony 11, 18, 19, 21
Connecticut, Fundamental Orders of 12
Connecticut River 6, 9, 11, 29, 42, 46, 67
Connecticut Valley 46, 47
Constitution, (USS *Constitution*) 27, 42, 44, 46, 50
Continental Congress 32
Corporal punishment 16

D

Damariscotta, Maine 28
Dana, Richard Henry 51
Dartmouth College 28
Daughters of Liberty 30
Davenport, Thomas 52
Dawes, William 78
Dedham, Massachusetts 74
Deer Island, Boston Harbor 76
Defense industry 42
Deforestation 61
Dermer, Thomas 6
Dewey, John 58
Dickinson, Emily 50
Dix, Dorothea 44
Dodge, Nehemiah 41
Dominion of New England 20
Dorr, Thomas 55
Dover, New Hampshire 22
Draper Company 81
Dublin, New Hampshire 48
Duryea, Charles and Frank 63
Dustin, Hannah 23
Dyer, Mary 17

E

Eddy, Mary Baker 63
Education 13, 48, 53
Edwards, Jonathan 27
Electric motor 52
Eliot Bible 75
Eliot, John 5, 9, 15, 73, 74
Elizabeth Islands 4
Embargo Act 45
Emerson, Ralph Waldo 44, 47, 52, 59, 60, 81, 82
Endicott, John 8
Environmental Movement 69
Epidemics 72
Erie Canal 49
Ether 57

F

Fairlee, Vermont 42

Fall River, Massachusetts 66
Falmouth, Maine 36
Falmouth, Massachusetts 17
Farming 61
Flu epidemic 66
Football 61
Forbush, Edward Howe 67
Fort Dummer, Vermont 25
Fort Ticonderoga 35
Fort William and Mary 32
Foxwoods casino 69
Freedom of religion 19
Freeport, Maine 66
French and Indian Wars 22, 28, 29, 77
French, Daniel Chester 60
Frost, Robert 62
Fruitlands 55, 82
Fuller, Margaret 52

G

Gage, General Thomas 32, 77
Garrison, William Lloyd 51
Gaspee Affair 31
Gay Rights Movement 70
Georgian architecture 25
Glaciation 1
Glorious Revolution 22
Gloucester, Massachusetts 5, 7, 25
Goodyear, Charles 56
Gorges, Fernando 8, 11
Grafton, Massachusetts 75
Graham, Sylvester 42
Granite Railway 50
Great Awakening 27
Great Swamp Fight 19
Greely, Alice 36
Green Mountain Boys 30
Green Mountain Club 65
Gun violence 71

H

Hadley, Massachusetts 18
Hall, Samuel 48
Hampden, Maine 44
Handel and Haydn Society 47
Hanover, New Hampshire 28
Hartford, Connecticut 11, 17, 18, 41, 46, 48, 57, 58, 60, 61
Harvard College 11, 47, 57, 58, 82; medical school 52
Harvard, Massachusetts 38, 64, 82
Haverhill, Massachusetts 23
Hawthorne, Nathaniel 42, 44, 58, 81, 82
Haynes, John 12
Hepburn, Katherine 67
Holmes, Oliver Wendell 50
Homer, Winslow 53
Hooker, Thomas 11
Hopedale Community 81
Howe, Colonel Thomas 22
Howe, Elias 57
Hudson, Henry 6
Huguenots 21
Hull, Isaac 46
Hull, John 16
Hunt, Thomas 6, 72
Hurricane Connie 68
Hurricane Diane 68
Hurricane, Great New England 68
Hutchinson, Anne 11

I

Ice 62
Ice Age 1, 72
Immigration; Irish 56, 65
Industrial revolution 40, 42, 46, 80
Insurance industry 42
International Monetary Conference 68
Interstate 95 69
Intolerable Acts 31, 77
Iron industry 27
Iroquois 2, 24
Isle au Haut 66
Isle La Motte 19

J

James I 5
Jewelry industry 41
Jewish colonists 17, 29
Jones, John Paul 37

K

Kennebec River 5, 36, 58
Kennedy, John F. 66, 69
Kidd, Captain 23
King Charles I 18
King Charles II 18
King George's War 27, 28
King James II 20, 22
King Louis XIV 21
King Philip's War 19, 75, 76
King William's War 23
Kittery, Maine 37

L

Labor Movement 49, 55, 59, 66; Ten hour workday 49
Lake Champlain 6, 19
Lake Cochituate 57
Lake Winnepesaukee 58
Larcom, Lucy 48
Lee, Ann 32, 38
Lexington, Massachusetts 78
Libraries 48
Lighthouses 26
Littleton, Massachusetts 75
Log drives 58
Londonderry, New Hampshire 26
Longfellow, Henry Wadsworth 42, 45
Long Trail 65
Long Wharf 27
Louisbourg 28
Lowell 56
Lowell, Francis Cabot 46, 80
Lowell, James Russell 58
Lowell, Massachusetts 47, 48, 75, 80
Lyceum movement 50
Lyon, Mary 53

M

Maine 20, 22; capital changes 51
Mann, Horace 53
Marlborough, Massachusetts 22, 75
Martha's Vineyard 1, 4
Mason, John 8
Massachusetts Bay Colony 8, 9, 19, 73
Massachusetts Bay Company 8
Massachusetts, constitution of 38
Massachusetts General Court 10
Massachusetts General Hospital 57
Massachusetts Institute of Technology 66
Massachusetts (Native American group) 15, 72
Massasoit 4, 7, 18, 73
Mather, Cotton 26
Mayflower 7
McKay, Donald 56
Merrimack River 8, 57, 73, 80
Metacomet 18, 76
Miantinomi 11
Middlesex Canal 44
Miller, William 56
Minute Man National Historical Park 82
Minute Man Statue 60
Minute Men 34, 78
Mohawks 12
Mohegans 11
Molasses Flood 66
Momaguin 12
Monhegan Island 46
Moody, Paul 80
Morey, Samuel 42
Morse, Samuel 56
Morton, William 57
Mountain lions 61
Mount Desert Island 5, 66
Mount Holyoke College 53
Mount Washington 13, 59, 64, 67
Mount Washington Hotel 65, 68
Mumford, Ann 75
Mystic, Connecticut 11

Mystic Seaport 54

N

Naismith, James 63
Nantucket 1, 25, 40
Narragansett, Rhode Island 28
Narragansetts 11, 73
Natick, Massachusetts 15, 74, 76
Naval War College 61
Neponset River 30
Netherlands 6
New Bedford, Massachusetts 40, 54
Newfoundland 25
New Hampshire 46
New Haven Colony 12, 13, 18
New Haven, Connecticut 24, 50, 56
New Light churches 27
New Netherland 19
Newport, Rhode Island 17, 29, 31, 61, 63
New York 13, 19
Nightclub fires 68, 70
Nipmucks 72, 73
Nonantum, Massachusetts 73
Nourse, Henry 64
Nova Scotia 25, 29
Nuclear power 69

O

Old Manse, Concord, Mass. 44, 52, 82
Old North Bridge, Concord 78
Old North Church 78
Old South Meeting House 27, 77
Old Sturbridge Village 51
Olmsted, Frederick Law 48

P

Paleo-Indians 1
Parker, Captain John 34, 78
Parkman, Dr. George 57
Pawtucket (Native American group) 72
Pawtucket, Rhode Island 40, 49

Peabody, Elizabeth 52
Peabody Museum 43
Peabody, Sophia 82
Penobscot Bay 6
Penobscot Expedition 38
Penobscot River 58
Pepperell, William 28
Pequot War 11
Philip, Wampanoag leader 18
Phillips Academy 38
Pierce, Franklin 42
Pilgrims 7, 73
Pine tree shillings 16
Pirates 23
Piscataqua River 7, 8
Pitcairn, Major John 34, 78
Plymouth Colony 4, 5, 6, 7, 8
Plymouth, Massachusetts 5, 6, 7, 72
Popham Beach, Maine 5
Portland Gale 64
Portland, Maine 22, 36, 45, 46, 48, 53, 58, 59
Portsmouth, New Hampshire 18, 20, 32, 43, 65
Preble, Commodore Edward 44
Prescott, Dr. Samuel 34, 78
Pring, Martin 5
Providence Plantation 11
Providence, Rhode Island 29, 30, 31, 32, 41
Puritans 8, 9, 15, 17, 73
Pynchon, William 11

Q

Quabbin Reservoir 57
Quakers 17, 52; execution of 17
Queen Anne's War 24, 25
Quincy Market 50
Quincy, Massachusetts 50

R

Racism 52
Railroads 44, 50, 54, 57, 60; Bangor & Piscataquis 52; Boston and

Worcester 52; Boston & Lowell 52; Boston & Providence 52; Boston & Worcester Railroad 52; Cog at Mount Washington 59; effect of 64; Granite Railway 50; Hartford & New Haven 50, 52; Nashua & Lowell 52; New York & New Haven 54; Westem Railroad 52; Wester 52
Red Cross, American 61
Regicide judges 18
Religious freedom 22
Revere, Paul 27, 29, 31, 33, 38, 42, 47, 77, 78
Rhode Island 15, 18, 24; William Blackstone moves to 73
Richardson, Henry Hobson 61
Ripley, George and Sophia 52, 54, 80
Roxbury Latin School 15
Roxbury, Massachusetts 9, 15, 73

S

Sabbathday Lake, Maine 32
Sagadahoc Colony 5
Salem, Massachusetts 8, 9, 22, 23, 39, 40, 43, 73
Salisbury, Connecticut 27, 48
Sandford, Frank W. 65
Sandy Hook Elementary School 71
Sassacus 12
Sassafras 4, 5
Saugus Ironworks 15
Sequasson 11
Sewall, Samuel 26
Sewing machine 57
Sex 53
Shakers 32, 38
Shawmut Peninsula 9, 73
Shays, Daniel 39
Shays' Rebellion 39
Sheep 54, 55; Marino 44
Shipbuilding 16, 25, 42, 56
Shoe industry 64

Singer, Isaac 57
Skiing 67
Slater, Samuel 80
Slavery 41, 44, 58, 60
Smallpox 26
Smith, John 6, 72
Snowstorms, notable 58, 62
Society for the Propagation of the Gospel in New England 75
Sons of Liberty 77
Springfield Armory 42
Springfield, Massachusetts 39, 42, 61, 63
Squanto 6, 7, 72, 73
St. Albans, Vermont 59
Stamp Act 30, 77
Stark, General John 36
Stark, New Hampshire 37
Steam transportation 42, 44, 50, 52, 54, 64
St. George's River 5
St. John River 54
St. Lawrence River 6
Stowe, Harriet Beecher 60
Strawbery Banke 7
Subway 64
Sudbury, Massachusetts 25
Sudbury River 57

T

Technology 62
Telegraph 56
Telephone 60, 61
Terrorism 70, 71
Textile industry 40, 41, 46, 49, 57, 66
Thomas, Robert Bailey 41
Thomson, David 7
Thoreau, Henry David 47, 52, 56, 59, 83
Tilden, William 74
Tobacco 15, 46
Tornado, Worcester 68
Touro Synagogue 29
Townshend Acts 30, 77

Transcendentalism 52, 56, 80, 82
Treaty of Ghent 47
Treaty of Paris 29
Tremont Street 73
Trinity Church 61
Trinity College 48
Trolleys 62
Turkeys, wild 20
Twain, Mark 60
Two Years Before the Mast 51
Typewriters 62

U

Uncle Tom's Cabin 60
Underground railroad 58
Union Oyster House 50
Unitarianism 48
United Colonies of New England 13
United States Constitution 40
Ursuline Convent 52
U. S. Coast Guard 39
Utopian communities 53, 55

V

Vermont 19, 29
Verrazzano, Giovanni da 4
Volleyball 64

W

Waban 73, 74
Wachusett Reservoir 57
Walden Pond 56, 83
Waltham, Massachusetts 46, 80
Wampanoags 7, 18, 19, 72, 73
War of 1812 46
Washington, George 35, 40, 79
Wayside Inn 25, 45
Weather 38, 47, 58, 61, 67, 68
Webster, John White 57
Webster, Noah 38
Wentworth, Benning 29
Wethersfield, Connecticut 16
Weymouth, George 5
Whaling 25, 40, 54

Wheatley, Phyllis 27
White Mountains 5, 60
Whitney, Eli 41, 43
Williams, Eunice 24
Williams, Roger 10, 11, 12, 15, 19
Winooski River 67
Winslow, Edward 9
Winthrop, John 9, 73
Winthrop, Jr., John 15, 18
Witch trials 22, 23
Women, status of 27, 36, 52, 57
Woods Hole Oceanographic Institution 67
Woodstock, Vermont 67
Wood, William 73
Worcester, Massachusetts 57, 68

Y

Yale College 24, 58
York, Maine 32
Youthful offenses 19, 26

www.ingramcontent.com/pod-product-compliance
Lightning Source LLC
Chambersburg PA
CBHW070632300426
44113CB00010B/1745